Praise for "The Giving Family"

"*The Giving Family* provides wonderful suggestions on how to teach children the importance of giving from a very young age and to make service part of a family's heritage."

— Marian Wright Edelman
President, Children's Defense Fund

"Using common sense, and without shouting, this book offers smart advice about how to teach children the value of charitable giving. There is no false piety here, no pretension; just good thinking and genuine humanity."

— Paul Newman

"This book will jog families to think about our responsibility as parents to instill a sense of altruism in our children. We are a fortunate nation and we need to share our privilege with the 25 percent of children who are below the poverty line."

— T. Berry Brazelton
Professor Emeritus, Pediatrics
Harvard Medical School

THE GIVING FAMILY:
Raising Our Children to Help Others

THE GIVING FAMILY:
Raising Our Children to Help Others

Susan Crites Price

Council on Foundations
1828 L Street, NW
Washington, DC 20036

Mission

The Council on Foundations is a membership organization that serves the public good by promoting and enhancing responsible and effective philanthropy.

Vision

In an environment of unprecedented change and potential, the Council on Foundations in the twenty-first century supports philanthropy worldwide by serving as

A trusted leader: Promoting the highest values, principles and practices to ensure accountability and effectiveness in philanthropy.

An effective advocate: Communicating and promoting the interests, value and contributions of philanthropy.

A valued resource: Supporting learning, open dialogue and information exchange about and for philanthropy.

A respectful partner: Collaborating within a network of philanthropic and other organizations working to promote responsible and effective philanthropy.

Statement of Inclusiveness

The Council on Foundations was formed to promote responsible and effective philanthropy. The mission requires a commitment to inclusiveness as a fundamental operating principle and calls for an active and ongoing process that affirms human diversity in its many forms, encompassing but not limited to ethnicity, race, gender, sexual orientation, economic circumstance, disability and philosophy. We seek diversity in order to ensure that a range of perspectives, opinions and experiences are recognized and acted upon in achieving the Council's mission. The Council also asks members to make a similar commitment to inclusiveness in order to better enhance their abilities to contribute to the common good of our changing society.

© 2001 Council on Foundations
Council on Foundations
1828 L Street, NW, Suite 300
Washington, DC 20036-5160
202/466-6512
www.cof.org

Dedication

Dedicated to children—blessed with the certainty that they can make the world a better place.

And dedicated to you—the adults who care for them. May you share in your children's conviction, energy and compassion, just as you demonstrate your own.

If together you give of your time, talent and treasure, the world will be a better place.

Table of Contents

Acknowledgments

To the author, who has gathered inspiring tales of philanthropic families and dedicated her career to helping parents guide their children.

To the Council on Foundations' Committee on Family Foundations, for giving voice to the needs of philanthropic families.

To the peer reviewers, whose life experience and vision shaped this volume, bringing it to a far wider segment of the public:

T. Dalbey, Jr., Trustee
Marie C. and Joseph C. Wilson Foundation

Sue Frueauff, Trustee and Program Officer
Charles A. Frueauff Foundation

Tracy Gary, coauthor
Inspired Philanthropy

Catherine Gund, Trustee
The George Gund Foundation

Susan Howbert, Director, Family Philanthropy Services
Council of Michigan Foundations

Tony Vitale, Trustee
The Lumpkin Foundation

— Karen Green
Managing Director, Family Foundation Services
Council on Foundations

Foreword

A teenager inspires her classmates to raise enough money to rent three trucks to ship supplies to Kosovo refugees . . . a child hosts a birthday party where the gifts are designated for homeless children . . . sisters and brothers put part of their allowance into a "family foundation" and, around the dinner table, decide how to give their money away.

These are great kids, growing up with the right values. And these are real stories unearthed by author Susan Price as she talked with young people and families around the country. You'll read about more of these young people throughout *The Giving Family: Raising Our Children to Help Others*.

But as an adult who cares for young people, you'll find something even more important in these pages. These children didn't acquire such deep commitment on their own. They were shown the way by parents, teachers, religious leaders and other adults. This book guides you through that process so you can bring out those values in your own family or in other children you care about.

There is no other book like this—full of practical, easy, family-oriented tips to help your children embrace the value of giving to others. From "gleaning" families visiting harvested fields to collect leftover crops for food banks to New York City's Penny Harvest, where school children and their families raise thousands of dollars in pennies for charity, these activities add a new dimension to family life.

When a family is committed to something larger than its own members, that commitment elevates the family and everyone in it. A brother and sister who fight over toys will learn instead to work together for a greater cause. Children who "need" the latest of every clothing fad will see their abundance in a larger perspective. Parents and children will discover new and deeper concepts to talk about.

In working with your children:

1. Be a role model—a volunteer and a donor.
2. Show kids the way—take them with you to volunteer; talk to them about your donations.
3. Make giving a year-round project, not just something to do at holidays.
4. Start now. The earlier you teach the habit of giving, the easier it will be to sustain.
5. Expect your children to serve and give.
6. Let children decide what projects to support with their money and time.
7. Teach them to manage money.
8. Praise them for their philanthropic actions.

The Council on Foundations works hard to help keep the family in family philanthropy. The Council commissioned this book as part of an effort to help families who form foundations pass the philanthropic impulse on to their children—and their children's children.

What came of this book, though, was something that reaches out to a much broader audience. Whether your family is affluent, comfortable or struggling, your family life and your children will grow stronger from the ideas in this book about giving—be it time, money or both—to others.

Here's an example: There is a youth program in rural and impoverished New Mexico, in which students who themselves were quite needy had adopted a school in an African country. When they learned that their "sister and brother students" had no books to read, the American students, on their own, came up with the idea to write and illustrate books for these children. The program obtained funds to publish these new authors. They are connected in a very personal way to young people an ocean away—and their own reading and writing have improved. Children who gain this kind of confidence—confidence that they can make a difference—will be able to draw on that sense of personal efficacy for the rest of their lives.

You will enjoy reading this book. Take to heart the inspiring stories of the generosity of young people that follow . . . and think about how your own family can start on the journey of giving that this book lays out for us so clearly and compellingly. There's no telling how far you and your children can go.

Dorothy S. Ridings
President and CEO
Council on Foundations

CHAPTER ONE

Charity Really Does Begin at Home: Nurturing a Family Tradition of Giving

Youth will be helped to believe that they can cope, and that, if they work at it over a lifetime, they may leave a little corner of the world a bit better than they found it.

—ROBERT K. GREENLEAF

Children learn to give from a young age. It is delightful for a parent when a child starts to outgrow the self-absorption of infancy and starts to mimic caring behavior—hugs, kisses, pats on the back and other simple recognitions of others.

In his book *Raising a Child with a High EQ* (HarperPerennial, 1998), Lawrence Shapiro notes that most toddlers intuitively try to reduce another child's distress, although they aren't sure exactly what to do. By six, children have the ability to see things from another person's perspective and act accordingly.

Parents work hard to build on this natural empathy that all children are born with. Every family has its traditions and its own ways to teach children to respect the needs of others and do kind things. As a child gets older, parents' efforts to instill the value of caring grow with the child. Sharing with others becomes an important skill as children enter school. Children's worlds expand in the school years, when they learn that there are many kinds of people and families in many kinds of communities.

When children approach high school, they begin to gain a fuller appreciation of the world and the social and economic problems many of us struggle with. They also start to form their own ideas about such issues and perhaps even develop an interest in a particular cause. With money of their own, they can make decisions about how to spend it.

This chapter will help you strengthen your own efforts to raise caring children during all of these stages of child and youth development. Children for whom "charity begins at home" have the world opened up for them.

Modeling the Values of Caring and Sharing

Ask almost any dedicated philanthropist the best way to impart philanthropic values to children and the answer likely to come back is "be a role model for them." Kids need to know that it's important to you that they are kind and giving. You teach them every time you talk to them about how to treat others and when you demonstrate compassionate behavior yourself.

Let your children see you give your time and talents. In her book *The Measure of Our Success: A Letter to My Children and Yours* (HarperCollins, 1993), Marian Wright Edelman, founder of the Children's Defense Fund, recalls the message she received from her parents beginning in early childhood: "We learned that service is the rent we pay for living. It is the very purpose of life and not something you do in your spare time." Let your children witness your giving too. Establishing the habit of giving with a preschooler can be the beginning of a lifelong commitment to generosity. Children notice when you place money in a collection plate, for example. They may ask if they can have the honor too.

Besides modeling caring behavior, take the next step. Actively teach your children about giving and your philanthropic values. Try some of the activities suggested in the rest of the chapter to start your child's philanthropic education.

Beginning the Discussion about Charitable Giving

The earliest lessons about giving have to be simple. For instance, if you buy a turkey for a needy family at Thanksgiving, explain that people who don't have enough money to buy things sometimes need our help. Explain the origin of the holiday too—that in 1621, Native Americans and Plymouth colonists gave thanks for a good harvest by joining together in an outdoor feast to which everyone contributed food.

Or the next time you're looking for a conversation-starter on a car trip, ask your kids, "If you had a million dollars to give away to deserving causes or people, whom would you give it to?" Be sure to ask the follow-up question, "Why?" You might learn a lot about your children's interests and concerns. After the kids have had turns, share some of your own thoughts about how you'd disburse such a sum. And if your family trip takes you to a scenic spot, talk about how important it is to protect the environment. If you tour a historic site supported by donations, explain to your children how the site is maintained.

---

activity

Find-Your-Talent Game

Adapted from *Teaching Children Responsibility* by Richard and Linda Eyre (Fireside, 1994).

1. With your children or any group of children, list each child's talents on a big sheet of paper.
2. Tell the kids to pick one of these talents and imagine the most wonderful use for it. For example, a child who is musical might be imagined as an adult on the stage at Carnegie Hall playing a benefit concert for a worthy cause.
3. As one person describes that scene, the others have to guess who is being discussed.

Remind your kids that, whether or not they have much money, they can use their talents to help people. Every family has stories of relatives who did something to serve the community—ran for office, headed the PTA, helped a neighbor, rallied for a cause. Tell those stories to your children so they understand that community involvement is part of your family's history. And when your kids talk about what they want to be when they grow up—a firefighter, for example—ask how they could help people if they had that kind of job, suggest Linda and Richard Eyre in their book *Teaching Children Responsibility* (Fireside, 1994). "Help your child see that the most important reason for choosing a particular career is that you can contribute something to others," they advise.

Read Me a Story

Many children's books offer wonderful lessons about sharing and caring. The Aesop fable *The Lion and the Mouse* and the more contemporary *The Rainbow Fish,* by Marcus Pfister (North-South Books, 1992), are just two examples for younger children. Older children can appreciate stories about famous—and not-so-famous—philanthropists, social activists and extraordinary volunteers. See the Resources section at the end of this book for a few suggested titles. Your librarian should be able to recommend others.

 TIP: Remember the story "Stone Soup"? At your next family or neighborhood gathering, try fixing a dinner by starting with a large pot, a clean stone and some water. Have each guest bring a contribution for the pot: vegetables, meat, spices, broth and so forth. Read the story aloud together and then involve everyone in preparing the meal. Younger children can decorate place mats, fold napkins and set the table. Older ones can cut up vegetables or bake biscuits to go with the stone soup.

<hr>

activity

Story Discussion

(Adapted from the Council of Michigan Foundations K–12 Education in Philanthropy Project)

Here's an example of how to explore the philanthropic theme of a storybook with your child:

Read the fable *The Lion and the Mouse.* You probably remember the story of the mouse who awakens a sleeping lion. The beast decides to let the mouse go and the mouse promises to do a favor for the lion. Later, when the lion is caught in a trap, the mouse gnaws the ropes to help him escape.
Then ask:

— Can you think of an example of when you have done something nice for another person?
— What is a trap?
— How did the mouse free the lion?
— Why couldn't the lion free himself?
— What lesson does the story convey? (Help your child relate the moral of the story to good citizenship. Ask about other kinds of good deeds citizens can do.)

<hr>

Using the Media to Your Advantage

The media provide other opportunities for teaching children the value of philanthropy. For example, probably every preschooler has learned something about caring for others by watching *Sesame Street or Mister Rogers' Neighborhood.* Videos such as Disney's *The Fox and the Hound* show kids that differences can be overcome if people—or animals—truly care for one another. Older kids might take inspiration from renting the classic film *Lilies of the Field,* in which Sidney Poitier is conned into building a church for destitute nuns. Watching television or movies with your kids and talking with them afterward about their reactions will enhance their experience.

Television can be another teaching tool. For example, although the news can be disturbing to children, it also can inspire them to help others. The devastating spring floods in Mozambique in 2000 produced vivid footage of whole families clinging to treetops and waiting for rescue. News reports on the conflict in Kosovo showed how children were forced to live in refugee camps. Both events spurred compassion and action by American children, who collected school supplies, toys, clothes and money to help the child victims of war and weather.

Anthropologist Jane Goodall tells a story of a five-year-old who had learned of Goodall's work with orphan chimpanzees from a National Geographic television special. The girl, named Amber Mary, approached Goodall after a lecture in Florida, clutching a stuffed Snoopy dog in one hand and a small bag of pennies in the other. In the television documentary, one chimp dies from grief after losing his mother. Amber Mary knew something about grief

---

activity

Make a Helping-Others Scrapbook

Start a scrapbook and add to it periodically:

— Collect magazine articles, news stories, pictures and other items that show people being helped or needing help.
— Use a page to jot down favorite children's books with "helping" themes.
— Include a list of special things the children say or do to help others or give to others. Update the list occasionally.
— As your children get older, you can include a list of groups or places in the community that your family is interested in helping or places you have helped in the past and want to visit again.

because her own brother had died of leukemia the year before. By saving her allowance for weeks, she was able to buy the toy dog, and she asked Goodall to give it to one of the orphan chimps to keep it company at night. The extra pennies were for bananas.

Passing on Your Giving Values through Family Rituals

Children thrive on rituals. Family celebrations, for example, are prime opportunities to create philanthropic traditions. To honor a child's birthday you might plant a tree. For Mother's Day, help your children do a good deed for someone else's mother whose children can't be with her. Family reunions, Grandparents' Day or religious holidays can all be occasions to celebrate the spirit of giving.

Incorporating Cultural Traditions

Your family may already have established giving rituals based on your culture and those of others. Use those traditions to re-inforce your message of giving. At some Chinese-American weddings, for example, the family of the groom presents a donation to a representative of a nonprofit community organization such as a hospital, school or senior center. Sometimes the parents of the bride match it. Jewish children often donate to charity a percentage of the money they receive on the occasion of their bar or bat mitzvahs. And African-American families who celebrate Kwanzaa sometimes recite a pledge written by author Maya Angelou: "We pledge to bind ourselves to one another, to embrace our lowliest, to educate our illiterate, to feed our starving, to clothe our ragged, to do all good things, knowing that we are more than the keeper of our brothers and sisters. We *are* our brothers and sisters."

Singer-songwriter and educator Buffy Sainte-Marie, founder of the Nihewan Foundation for American Indian Education, describes a Native American tradition called a Giveaway. "A Giveaway is usually held to share and acknowledge something good that has

---

Exposing Kids to Philanthropy at a Young Age

Larry Lowe, a third generation Chinese American, attends many fundraising dinners to support Chinese social service institutions in the San Francisco Bay area. He and his wife take along their four- and seven-year-old children to expose them to the need "to support the community from which you came." In this way, he is passing on a family tradition. When he was young, his parents took him and his siblings to a large restaurant in Chinatown several times a year for fundraising dinners.

Lowe admits that these evenings were boring for kids and he didn't enjoy them, but he believes they had a lot to do with instilling the philanthropic values that he imparts today to his own kids. And he's working to make the fundraisers he's involved in more family-friendly and fun for the younger set.

---

happened, such as improved health, harvest or the birth of a child," she explains. An individual or family calls friends and relatives together and presents them all with gifts. If the Giveaway is to honor a toddler or other child, the parents will hold the event on their child's behalf and enlist the child's help in passing out the gifts and greeting each recipient, thanking them for coming. "The Giveaway serves both a social function and an economic function," Sainte-Marie adds. Besides being a fun occasion, "a Giveaway is one more Native American way to redistribute wealth, goods, services and happiness."

Variations on Gift Giving

Gift-giving days and rituals are perfect opportunities to demonstrate your charitable values. Like many parents, Ellen Sloan of

Santa Monica, California, worried that her young children received too many presents at holiday times and birthdays. For her younger child's second birthday, Sloan threw a big party. Both of Sloan's children were adopted from China, so she suggested that the guests donate to a charity that cares for Chinese orphans, rather than purchase gifts for her child.

And when her oldest turned four, Sloan asked her daughter's friends to bring an unwrapped toy or book suitable for any age and either sex. The main party activity was making wrapping paper using finger painting, stamps and markers. Then the kids wrapped the gifts and Sloan took them to local free clinic to distribute to families in need. The kids had a great time and the clinic sent them thank-you letters. The birthday girl was content with the gifts she received from her family.

 TIP: When you and your children buy gifts for friends and family, you can also help your favorite charities. Gift shops at your local zoo, aquarium or historic site, and catalogues from the Smithsonian Institution, UNICEF and many other groups, provide an array of gift items with proceeds going to support the organizations. Some Web sites will let your family designate a charity to receive a percentage of what you spend. Target, for example, has a plan that sends 1 percent to your child's school.

Planting the Seed

Children's interest in philanthropy may wax and wane through the years. A child who's very active in volunteer efforts and charitable giving in elementary or middle school may show less interest in high school, when homework, sports and social life take all his energies. It's common for one child in a family to be very philanthropic while another shows no interest at all. It's best to let all your children go at their own pace. Provide opportunities without pressure and tailor those opportunities to fit the interests of each child.

story

Donating in the Name of Others

John Davis of Springfield, Massachusetts, remembers that his grand-mother didn't send Christmas and birthday presents to her grandchil-dren. She felt their parents had adequately provided for them. Instead, the grandkids received letters saying "You'll be happy to know I've sent a donation in your name to. . ." and listing the charity. "This stuck out in my mind," Davis recalls, and made him feel involved in helping needy people through his grandmother. "She had been an orphan and always had an interest in people who were having hard times," he says. Davis remembers that when she was 90, his grandmother was walking by a daycare center at a church and heard children "who sounded like angels." Soon after, she received a misdelivered milk bill intended for the center totaling $500. She paid it. "She taught us by her example," Davis says.

It's also not unusual for young people to quietly absorb the lessons of youth but not to act on them until they become parents themselves. Just as children who attend religious services with their families may turn away from religion in early adulthood and then return when they have children of their own, so, too, young parents often want to set the example of compassion that their parents set for them.

As with most child-rearing matters, the more you push philan-thropy, the more your children may resist. You can't force kids to have a philanthropic spirit. The best approach is to talk about caring and sharing, model those values in your own life and give them opportunities to participate when they are ready. If you do that, you'll have planted the seeds for the next generation of givers.

CHAPTER TWO

The Family That Volunteers Together: Encouraging Children to Give Their Time

The health of the family and the health of society are interlinked. And family volunteerism is one very profound way to preserve both.

–LEE SALK, CHILD PSYCHOLOGIST AND AUTHOR

Helping your children share their time and talents can be one of the most rewarding things you do as a parent. The payoffs—for children, parents and the community—are many.

Volunteering is one of the best ways to build a child's character and self-esteem. Children who volunteer acquire new skills, develop confidence and maturity, put their own problems in perspective, meet people from other backgrounds and learn teamwork and civic responsibility. Research shows that youth who volunteer are also less likely to engage in risky behavior such as drug use and sexual activity. Experts say that teaching children compassion can head off violent or hurtful behavior. Some kids may even be led to a career path through their volunteer work.

For families, volunteering is a good way to spend quality time together, to share experiences, establish traditions and have fun, all while helping the community. Family volunteer work can create a strong bond, helping family members communicate with and be supportive of each other.

From the community's point of view, young people are a valuable resource for nonprofit organizations that have seen their volunteer ranks shrink as more women entered the work force. Teenagers, especially, are being looked upon as a key resource for sustaining volunteer-dependent efforts. Independent Sector, a national organization that encourages philanthropy and volunteering, reports that in 1996 teenagers volunteered at a higher rate than adults. Fifty-nine percent of teens aged 12 to 17 said they volunteered at least 3.5 hours per week, often through religious institutions or schools. Teens who grew up with positive adult role models were nearly twice as likely to volunteer as those who did not.

When to Start

It's never too early to start taking your kids with you when you volunteer, as long as you are thoughtful about the kinds of work you tackle with the youngest of them. People in nursing homes, for example, love to hold babies, even crying ones who need comforting. But taking the baby along while you answer the phones at a crisis hotline has obvious drawbacks.

The big advantage of starting early is that it's easier to establish the volunteering habit in young children. It becomes a natural part of a child's life. And if your choice of volunteer activity involves direct services to people in need, your child will probably adapt easier if started at an early age. A child who accompanies parents on visits to nursing homes or soup kitchens—where even three-year-olds can be put in charge of napkin folding—will be more comfortable and confident in that setting than a child who starts such work a few years later.

Rebecca Wagner, who founded a shelter for homeless women in her Rockville, Maryland, church 20 years ago, often took her young sons with her when she served meals there. "They'd do their homework at the table, then eat their meals with the women and talk to them," she says. "It had a normalizing effect on the women because it triggered some sense of a regular life in them." And it helped her sons develop sensitivity to others.

Harvesting for the Hungry

A volunteer project that goes back to biblical times, gleaning, is a favorite activity for families such as the Gannons of Washington, DC. Every fall they harvest vegetables that are left in farmers' fields after the best of the crop has been shipped to supermarkets. Much edible produce remains; but because it wasn't ripe during the initial picking, or because of small imperfections, it would normally be left to rot. Instead, farmers open their fields to volunteers to gather the harvest for delivery to area food banks.

"We've been taking our kids since they were in backpacks," says Maureen Gannon, mother of four daughters, two of whom are now in college. "We've picked apples, cucumbers, peppers and squash. You see all this food that would just be plowed under and you can't believe how much you can harvest."

Her kids look forward to the annual outing. Families pack picnic lunches and enjoy the fresh autumn air, sunshine and socializing, as well as the hard work. The Gannons used to go with a group from their church, but now they've also brought in families from their daughters' school and from other organizations they belong to. "Last year we had about 150 people and it was really fun for everybody, including really little kids," she says.

 TIP: To find out about gleaning in your part of the country, call the U.S. Department of Agriculture's hotline, 800/GLEAN-IT. Or consider starting your own project.

Finding Family Volunteer Projects

The simplest projects can be found right in your neighborhood. A senior citizen may need help with yard work or grocery shopping, for example. Anywhere you look, you can probably find a person in need of assistance.

Other ideas for projects may come from groups you are affiliated with already, such as a religious institution or school. Many newspapers and city magazines list volunteer opportunities, and a variety of volunteer options can also be located through Internet sites. Some families make it a practice to volunteer for the local organizations they give money to. This lets their children see firsthand what the needs are and how contributions of both time and money can make a difference.

TIP: You can also contact the volunteer center in your community for ideas. There are nearly 500 of these around the country, some affiliated with United Way, others either independent or connected to another social service agency. The Points of Light Foundation, through its Family Matters program, maintains a hotline to connect callers with local volunteer centers in their community. (Call 800/VOLUNTEER. Also see the Resources section of this book for more information on locating volunteer opportunities.)

Although one-time events, such as a playground clean-up or a 10K walk, are worthwhile activities, a project a family undertakes regularly could have more meaning to a child. Some families take on continuing projects while also participating occasionally in single-event activities for variety or to help causes they are close to, such as their schools.

Be aware that many organizations prefer adult volunteers but will accept children who are accompanied by parents. Be sure to inquire about age requirements before you sign on to a project with your kids.

What's Appropriate at Which Ages

Some parents worry that their children will be upset or nervous by a volunteering activity that puts them in contact with people who are homeless, sick, disabled, or frail and elderly. "Kids take their cues from parents," says Wagner, who's now executive director of Community Ministry of Montgomery County, Maryland.

"If the parents act nervous, the kids are going to be and the folks they try to help will sense that." Wagner says comfort levels—for children and adults—improve with time and experience.

Wagner's agency gets its volunteers from faith congregations of many denominations. There's no minimum age for kids to volunteer in the organization's homeless shelter as long as they are with their parents. However, when groups of elementary kids attend, with their scout leaders for example, they are assigned tasks that don't involve direct contact with clients. They sort clothes in the clothing distribution center, make place mats, collect and wrap presents and run drives to collect toiletries.

Sheltering Kids vs. Exposing Them to the Needy

Deborah Spaide, founder of Kids Care Clubs, an organization that helps families engage in volunteer projects, warns that in an age of TV and the Internet "our greatest efforts to shelter kids aren't going to be successful. They will be exposed to suffering. They'll walk by a homeless person and want a way to respond. If we don't give that to them, they'll develop apathy."

She doesn't think families necessarily have to take their children to soup kitchens to make the point, but she believes parents should at least talk with their kids about others less fortunate. "Answer their questions and keep it simple. If they are concerned about people not having homes, ask what they think they could do."

Often, children will propose holding fundraisers—anything from lemonade stands to yard sales—to help the needy. While raising money is a worthy project in itself, children will get more out of it if they go beyond simply mailing a donation and become more directly connected with the cause they are supporting. "If children are involved in fundraising, we want them to complete the circle," Spaide says. For example, they can take their lemonade-stand proceeds and go with their parents to shop for food and deliver it to a soup kitchen.

Spaide, author of *Teaching Your Kids to Care* (Replica Books, 1995), also feels that at least some of a child's volunteer experiences should be directed to meeting human needs. While it's certainly rewarding for families in a middle-class neighborhood to raise funds and rebuild their school playground, for example, the participants are the ones who benefit. Spaide thinks children also need to be involved in activities that will help those less fortunate. "A necessary component of charity is the ability to feel someone else's pain." Taking the next step—doing something to help—empowers children.

If you're looking for projects that a group of kids can do, log on to **www.KidsCare.org**, where you'll learn how to start a Kids Care Club. The site offers an organizing handbook, project ideas, an e-newsletter and a support hotline for groups of kids, from preschoolers through high schoolers. A companion group, FamilyCares (**www.familycares.org**), provides ideas for dozens

---

story

Looking for Child- and Family-Friendly Programs

Deborah Spaide's interest in youth volunteerism began when she and her husband introduced their five children to the benefits of helping others. They spent an exhausting but fulfilling day sprucing up the public housing apartment of an elderly woman, who was extremely grateful. The kids enjoyed the experience so much that they told friends at school, and they wanted to get involved too. Spaide called around to find an agency in her Connecticut community that wanted the efforts of a gang of child do-gooders, but only two of the groups responded positively, and they just wanted kids to stuff envelopes. She found that many organizations preferred adults.

Since then, she's devoted herself "to opening the minds of organizations to the usefulness of kid volunteers." She works with groups such as the Red Cross and Meals on Wheels to develop programs that are child- and family-friendly.

of easy, inexpensive projects families can do together to help people who are homeless, elderly, disadvantaged or ill. Both resources are free to parents with Internet access (see the Resources section).

Your local Red Cross chapter is another place to check for volunteer projects. One of the organization's more popular activities with children is the 80-year-old School Chest program. The idea is to fill a chest, preferably a large plastic bin, with school supplies and playthings for 40 children. Last year, 300 chests filled by American children in schools, scout troops or other youth organizations were shipped to Kosovo refugees. Estimated costs for the project range from $280 to $450. Sometimes office supply stores will donate items. The Red Cross provides a list of items needed and detailed instructions. Check your phone book or visit the Web site **www.redcross.org** to find the chapter nearest you.

Family Matters

The Points of Light Foundation sponsors a National Family Volunteer Day around Thanksgiving each year. To keep the momentum going year-round, the foundation created the Family Matters initiative with funding from the W. K. Kellogg Foundation "to make family volunteering the norm in the United States," says Family Matters former Senior Director Eileen Cackowski.

"There was a cycle when women stopped volunteering and went back to work," Cackowski explains. "We've raised a generation of kids who were not taken along when their parents volunteered." She aims to change that by providing more volunteer opportunities in which parents can work alongside their children.

Cackowski required her own kids to volunteer. It wasn't a hard sell. "All they had to do was volunteer once, and they'd get hooked. Children are so free and open and they feel good when someone else feels good." Her children have continued volunteering as adults.

---

story

It's Never Too Early

Laura Kind McKenna is a nurse practitioner who volunteers one day a week at a free clinic in Philadelphia. Over the years, all four of her children have accompanied her to the clinic, performing simple tasks such as straightening the facility's lending library or parceling over-the-counter pain relievers and vitamin tablets into small bottles to be given to patients.

"But the volunteering is secondary," McKenna stresses. She took her children so they would "hear people's stories" and see what life is like for those without many resources. The clinic used to be located on top of a soup kitchen, and McKenna and her children sometimes ate there with other volunteers and with the clients, some of whom were mentally ill.

She doesn't think kids should be sheltered from volunteer work that might be a little disturbing to them. "Having a little discomfort isn't bad for kids," she says. "Actually, it enriches you." Otherwise, she adds, "you build up a fear of being around people who are poor. I was raised with a really strong message that we weren't better because we had more. This was an important value in our family. There's no age that's too early to convey this message to your children. All my kids have become involved in service projects and gotten a lot of satisfaction from it."

When picking projects, she advises, families should "learn what you like and what you don't like." The only way to learn is to try it. "Until you do, you don't know what you're capable of." But don't worry so much about the kids' reaction. She tells of a two-year-old tossing a beach ball with an elderly woman who has serious dementia. "The child doesn't know there's anything wrong, just that she has a new playmate who never gets tired of throwing the ball back."

Fitting Volunteering into the Schedule

Some agencies are finding that the only way to attract adult volunteers is to let them bring their children. What little free time parents have, they don't want to spend away from their kids. Even so, families have to work at finding slots in their schedules for volunteer work.

The ones who do manage to make time often adopt a systematic approach: Take a look at your monthly calendar and block in the hours that are committed already, to work, school, sports practices, PTA meetings and so forth. Look at the space left and decide what amount you want to give to volunteering—two hours on Saturday afternoon, for example, or two nights once a month. If there are no blocks of time, consider reprioritizing your commitments, noting what can be eliminated to allow for volunteering.

 TIP: It's possible to combine volunteering with a family vacation. For example, you may be able to link up with a church group that is rehabilitating houses in an impoverished area located near a part of the country—or another country—that you'd also like to tour. Spend part of your time working and the rest being a tourist.

After You've Volunteered

Your children will get a lot more out of their volunteer work if they talk about it afterward. Take some time to reflect on how each family member felt about the experience by asking questions like:

What did you like best? Least?
What did you learn that surprised you?
Did anything make you uncomfortable?
How do you think we could be even more effective?
Should we do this project again or try something new?

Don't forget to work in some praise at the end. Kids love to hear it, and they will be more likely to want to volunteer again if they feel their efforts are appreciated.

story

Mother-Daughter Philanthropy Club

You've probably heard of mother-daughter book clubs, but here's a twist. In San Diego, Valerie Jacobs Hapke and her ninth grade daughter, Claire, belong to a group called SPRITES (Spiritual, Philanthropic, Recreational, Inspirational, Training, Education and Social) that brings together 133 girls and their mothers for volunteer projects, fundraising and giving.

Started in 1968, the organization "strives to teach lifelong commitment to community service," Hapke says. Each year the group of seventh through twelfth graders donates 8,000 hours to a variety of organizations in San Diego County. The girls and mothers are invited to join by someone they know in the group. Each grade takes on a particular volunteer project for a year. The entire club also joins forces on other activities. The seventh and eighth graders work with Horsemanship for the Handicapped, which helps children with disabilities ride horses. Other projects have included visiting a children's hospital and hosting parties at a home for abused and neglected children. Mimicking the old-fashioned quilting bee, the girls and their moms made quilted lap robes for senior citizens. An annual fashion show serves as a fundraiser to support some of the groups that the families volunteer for.

"The group was created partly as a way for mothers and daughters to stay in communication through volunteering. It's a way to keep our relationships strong," Hapke explains. Not to be outdone, Hapke's high-school-age son and her husband volunteer at a soup kitchen every Sunday.

Hapke, who chairs the Jacobs Family Foundation, wants her children to be aware of their community's needs. Her family's foundation is building a commercial project that incorporates community development programs in a low-income neighborhood in San Diego. "We decided to move our offices into the neighborhood where we were working. When we have events, we have our kids come so they can see what's going on in that neighborhood." Through the foundation's work and their family volunteering, Hapke's kids have gotten an early education in philanthropy.

TIP: In chapter 1 we mentioned creating a "helping-others scrap-book" to get kids thinking about the subject. Once you start volunteering as a family, FamilyCares suggests, make a charity memory book using drawings or photographs to show who was helped. Include any thank-you notes received from the groups or individuals, and record your children's impressions of the experience and what they learned. Use the book to review past family volunteer work and talk about what the kids would like to do next.

Opportunities beyond the Family

As your children get older, their opportunities for volunteering move beyond those they do with the family. Groups that promote volunteering—scout troops, 4-H, religious institutions, schools—all can expand their reach. And they give your children a chance to team up with peers instead of parents.

Many of these organizations rely on parents for help in transporting kids or making arrangements with agencies to be served. So if you want your child to continue being a volunteer, it helps if you're one too. (For more about kids volunteering with peers, see chapter 3.)

Helping Older Kids Find the Right Volunteer Jobs

"Young people have a passion, and it's the role of adults to help them identify what that passion is," says Jim McHale, assistant vice president of the W. K. Kellogg Foundation. "If we think back to our childhood, we can all remember an adult—maybe a parent or a teacher—who got us involved in something we deeply care about."

Anne Hoover, executive director of Community Partnerships with Youth, urges you to encourage your older children to develop a personal mission statement. The statement may change over time, but it serves to focus the child on her current passion, whether it's the environment or the elderly. (It's a good exercise for parents too.)

---

activity

Creating a Personal Mission Statement

(Adapted from *Youth as Trustees*, a curriculum of Community Partnerships with Youth.)

A personal mission is developed by combining our beliefs, interests, skills and qualities with the needs we see around us in global or local communities. Start by finishing the following statements in your own words:

1. The world or my community needs people who . . .
2. I believe that . . . (to help your children identify their personal beliefs, ask them how Martin Luther King, Jr., Mother Teresa, Gloria Steinem or someone else they admire might complete this statement)
3. A cause I care deeply about is . . .
4. To give to my community and the world, I have these special skills and qualities (or would like to develop these skills or qualities) . . .

After filling in the blanks, your child should use these responses to write a brief mission statement that:

— reflects your child's values
— is lofty
— gives direction for your child's talents
— serves as a compass for personal decisions about where and how your child will serve the greater good.

Kids are more likely to stick with a volunteer activity if it's one they choose for themselves rather than one picked out by Mom and Dad. That doesn't mean you can't help the process along, however. Think about your child's skills and talents. Then do some research on organizations in your community whose needs match those skills.

Is your child a whiz with computers? Senior citizen centers may be desperately looking for volunteers who can introduce

TIP: Here is a partial list of causes to help your child identify one she cares about.

AIDS
Animals and wildlife
Anti-Semitism
Antiracism
Arts and humanities
Disaster relief
Drug and alcohol abuse
Education
Environment
Gun control
Health care and medical research
Hunger
Housing and homelessness
International concerns
Medical research
Mental health and crisis services
Recreation
Religion
Science
Women's rights
Youth development

seniors to computers and the Internet. Iona House in Washington, DC, has a cadre of high school students teaching computer skills to neighborhood seniors. After their training at Iona, the seniors become volunteers themselves, helping children enrolled in inner city after-school programs with their homework. Thus, the work of one teenager affects many lives.

The personal contact in computer volunteering is important. Deborah Spaide cautions that the local community, not the Internet, should be the venue for children's volunteer work. "Virtual volunteering" may be okay for adults, she says, but kids need a more in-person approach.

---

activity

Checklist: Choosing a Volunteer Project

Fill out this checklist to help you identify your interests, time requirements and skills. Then use the information to find a volunteer job that is a good match.

— List your hobbies, interests and skills. Would you like to use any of them in a volunteer job?
— Would you like to learn any new skills?
— Why do you want to be a volunteer?
— Have you done volunteer work before? What did you like or dislike about the experience?
— How much time do you have to offer?
— Do you want a short-term or long-term project?
— When do you want to volunteer? (Evenings? Weekends?)
— Do you enjoy working one-on-one with people, e.g., mentoring, tutoring?
— Do you prefer working with a group of volunteers?
— Do you like working outside or inside?

Next, research volunteer opportunities that fit the information from above:

— Do the missions of the organizations you are considering match your interests?
— How much of a time commitment do they require?
— Do their schedules fit yours?
— Will these projects fulfill your motivations for volunteering?

Kids who excel at sports are needed as assistant coaches for children with physical or mental disabilities. A teen with a pleasing voice and a love of books might enjoy recording books for the blind or reading to a blind neighbor. Those with musical or dramatic talent are always welcome to perform at nursing homes, senior centers or shelters. Teens with a knowledge of Spanish can tutor immigrants learning English or help organizations translate brochures into Spanish. A young person who loves animals can volunteer at an animal shelter or local zoo. A book lover can shelve books at the school or public library.

Teenagers may feel pressured if you try to steer them into a particular activity. That's why it's best if you simply act as a resource for your teenagers without being directive. Offer brochures or information you collect about community service opportunities, and your help (such as transportation) if they need it. Then stand back and let them decide which to choose. This doesn't mean you shouldn't expect your child to do some type of community service. Some families require children to do some volunteer work, perhaps over the summer or on weekends.

It might be a good idea for your child to sample some activities once or twice before making a regular commitment. Also, don't expect a young adolescent to pick one activity and stick with it throughout high school. Kids have short attention spans and like to experiment with new things. Let your kids rotate through several volunteer experiences during their school years, if that's their preference. Have your teen find out whether the agency she chooses has a commitment requirement, and make sure she's willing to stay with the job at least that long.

No job is right for all kids. A teenager who volunteers in a nursing home, for example, needs to be able to deal with the possibility that an elderly person she works with might die. Some kids love working with children but may find it stressful to deal with those who have serious mental or physical disabilities. Others will have no problem as long as the organization they work for has prepared them for what to expect.

 TIP: If you have college-age children who volunteer, they can earn frequent flyer miles on United. The airline, in partnership with America's Promise, awards 5,000 miles for every 50 hours of work performed for participating agencies. For more information, go to the Web site **www.CollegePlus.com**.

---

story

Three Generations of Family Volunteers

As a young girl, Lisa Landwirth Ussery knew her father, Henri Landwirth, was a Holocaust survivor. She'd seen an identification number tattooed on his arm. But she wasn't told much about his experience. By the time she reached high school, she came to know more about his story. He was imprisoned in a concentration camp during his teenage years, and the Nazis killed both his parents. "That had a huge impact on the direction of my life," cultivating her passion against prejudice and injustice, she says.

Ussery remembers being exposed to volunteering at an early age, particularly in Camp Fire, which she participated in from the age of 6 to 18. Her mother was a Pink Lady volunteer at a hospital. Almost every weekend, the family visited Maurice, who had been in the camps with her dad. "They saved each other's lives," Ussery says. Maurice lived in a dark apartment "and he was very disturbed by the war. We tried to keep him company."

Ussery pursued a career in social work and took a succession of jobs, with the U.S. Senate Committee on Aging, Big Brothers and Big Sisters, and a geriatric residential treatment center for disturbed elderly patients. She shifted gears when her two children were born, volunteering at a homeless shelter and handling prisoner correspondence

---

Using Volunteers Wisely

Most kids want meaningful volunteer work. They'll likely be bored with envelope-stuffing, no matter how worthwhile the ultimate goal. If they choose to volunteer in a daycare center because they like working with children, they'll feel exploited if all they get to do is clean paint pots or sweep the floor. When talking to an agency that is seeking student volunteers, ask questions about the volunteers' duties and find out how much adult supervision there will be.

for Amnesty International, something she was drawn to because of her dad's imprisonment.

Ussery is president of the Fanny Landwirth Foundation in Florida, which her father endowed and named for his mother. Her brothers Gary and Greg serve with her on the board and are also active with their own charities. Ussery is passing on her family legacy of helping the poor, the sick and the homeless. She has taken her older daughter, Sarah, aged nine, on site visits. She planned a mother-daughter sorting day to distribute new clothes purchased for homeless and foster children. She talks to her children about her philanthropic work, and involves them as well. "Doing things is important," she says, "not just on holidays but all year round."

Ussery's children also receive inspiration from their grandfather's active philanthropy. With his own funds and the support of others, he has built Give Kids the World, a magical village in Orlando where families of children with life-threatening illnesses can stay while visiting nearby Disney World.

In an office where she once worked, Ussery posted one of her father's favorite quotations by Winston Churchill for inspiration: "You make a living by what you get. You make a life by what you give."

CHAPTER THREE

You're Not in This Alone: Learning Philanthropy in the Community

Everyone can be great because everyone can serve.

—MARTIN LUTHER KING, JR.

Children can learn the importance of philanthropy and service in many places beyond the family. Although they still may enjoy family volunteer projects occasionally, most children, starting in elementary school, will prefer projects undertaken with peers.

Studies show that most youth volunteers are involved in structured activities. Independent Sector found that teens, when asked where they learned of service opportunities, cited religious institutions (64 percent), school (30 percent) and other groups (14 percent). Some of those same groups, especially religious institutions, teach the importance of donating money as well as time. These organizations can reinforce the philanthropic education you provide your children. When you encourage your children to join youth organizations, service clubs, religious groups or student government, you expand their opportunities to learn about sharing their time, talent and treasure with others.

Community Service through School

A growing number of schools—mainly junior high and high schools—provide students with community service opportunities. Some high schools require "service-learning" hours for graduation and link the service activities to the curriculum. Maryland was the first state to require all students to complete a certain number of hours of service-learning. The move became part of a long-running debate about whether schools should require service.

Proponents say part of a well-rounded education is learning civic responsibility, and that requiring service makes it more likely that students will find an interest, develop the habit and continue to volunteer when they are adults. Proponents add that service-learning enhances critical thinking skills and improves students' sense of competence and psychological maturity. But others say it's not truly volunteer work if it's required. Or they argue that community service distracts from academic coursework and is difficult for cash-strapped schools to implement.

Deborah Spaide of Kids Care is of two minds about this issue. "Kids who are required to do community service may later say, 'I'm so glad I did,'" Spaide notes. "They may end up choosing a career in social service." She points out that parents make their children brush their teeth to get them into the habit, so is making them do community service all that different? On the other hand, Spaide adds, "my understanding of philanthropy is that it's not volunteerism if you can't volunteer. I would rather it came from the heart. I wish schools would do more to track what kids are doing and reward it, but not require it."

Dwight Burlingame, associate executive director of the Indiana University Center for Philanthropy, argues that "the importance of the activity shouldn't be minimized. Requiring service doesn't take away from the experience itself, any more than requiring science courses takes away from the value of science." Burlingame considers the larger picture. "The tradition of philanthropy is in jeopardy. If you don't teach a tradition, you forget it." Children who grow up away from extended family members and whose parents have little time for volunteering because of work commitments are not as exposed to philanthropy as earlier generations were.

Regardless of where you stand on the requirement debate, the school setting is a logical place for students to learn about service opportunities. Long before there was service-learning, schools often had service clubs as extracurricular activities. The most effective programs provide support to students who volunteer. Support can include transportation to volunteer activities, free periods during the day so kids can leave the school to volunteer, and a staff person assigned to find opportunities and coordinate student participation.

Parent Input in Schools' Community Service Programs

If your school doesn't have a program and you think it should, you could raise the issue with your parent association. Often it is parent impetus that gets programs going, especially if parents are willing to help by researching opportunities and providing transportation. If your school does have community service opportunities, your input and assistance can make a good program better.

Requiring community service doesn't mean a school's program will be better than an optional program. Some schools that require service allow kids to earn credits just for performing simple tasks—sometimes in the school building—that have little connection to serving community needs.

Elements of a Good Service-Learning Program

To create a good learning experience in a service program, you must focus on the students from the beginning, says the Points of Light Foundation. The students should have a voice in the planning process. They need to be given proper training for each assignment. Time should be set aside for reflection, and students should evaluate their work (what they did well, what they could

---

story

The Landon School

Landon, a private boys' school with grades 3–12 in Bethesda, Maryland, has had a community service program for 33 years. Bob Condit, a chemistry teacher and guidance counselor, started it and still runs it today. Landon doesn't require community service. Yet 60 percent of its high schoolers, including almost all juniors and seniors, are involved in year-long service projects. The governor of Maryland has recognized it as one the state's outstanding programs for building self-esteem.

One of the secrets of Landon's success is student management. After paving the way with the agencies being served, Condit relies on student leaders to recruit other volunteers and keep the projects running smoothly. He never lacks for boys who want such leadership opportunities.

Service coordinators in coed schools tell him it's easier to get girls involved than boys. "You have to get past the threshold that it's an okay thing to do," Condit says. That's why he focuses on getting varsity athletes involved. Once students see the football quarterback mentoring a handicapped child, for example, community service becomes cool.

Support from the top helps too. When the head of Big Brothers attended an assembly to present an award to Landon, the principal declared that the honor made him as proud as if the school had won a football championship.

The array of service choices Landon provides—approximately 45— means there's something to meet every interest. The high schoolers are big brothers to kids who are fatherless, help elderly people care for their homes and yards, run athletic activities for children who are

---

have done better, whether they made a difference). And their efforts ought to be celebrated and recognized.

These elements should apply to projects your son or daughter tackles with any group of peers, not just projects through school. Some of the most important growth occurs when the students get

mentally or physically disabled, conduct recycling programs and maintain hiking trails. "You can never have too many programs," Condit stresses. If a student has an interest in a type of service not already offered, Condit helps him create a program.

Condit's approach has always been carrot and stick. He participates in a consortium of community service coordinators from several area private schools. Most require students to perform service. "When they say they want to increase the hours required so kids get more involved, I say, 'Why not focus instead on finding programs kids will want to volunteer for?'" Condit says agencies his school works with complain to him that the kids who come from programs requiring service often ask to have a schedule tailored to meet—but not exceed—the required hours.

Landon alumnus Alex Bush, now a sophomore at the University of Pennsylvania, is cochair in a major charity event sponsored by his fraternity. At Landon, the varsity athlete led a community service project that arranged weekly visits by 40 students to a school for children with mental disabilities. Bush says he'd spend time with his "little brother" in class and hang out with him on the playground. "We'd just talk. It was really fun."

Condit relies on parents to help with projects that take place on weekends. The school also organizes parent-son community service days. His only requirement is that the adults let the students run the show. "I'm a great advocate of student leaders," he says.

together to reflect on what they learned from the experience. You can support that process. Whenever your child does community service, with or without the family, ask questions that will encourage him to reflect.

Schools That Teach Philanthropy

Some schools go a step beyond community service by infusing their curriculum with lessons about the nonprofit sector and encouraging their students to become citizens who work for the common good.

One notable example is a curriculum developed for grades kindergarten through 12 by the Council of Michigan Foundations. Called the K–12 Education in Philanthropy Project, this detailed set of teacher-developed classroom lessons is used primarily in Michigan schools but is spreading to other states as well. Started with W. K. Kellogg Foundation funds and now supported by others as well, the program has the advantage of reaching all kids at a school, unlike programs run by religious institutions or youth groups.

The lessons, which have been field tested and evaluated, can be integrated into the academic content teachers are already using. "For example, everyone teaches about the Underground Railroad," says Kathryn Agard, the project director. "Our lesson talks about volunteers and the role they played in it. Students have been learning about philanthropy all along, they just hadn't named it."

Through the curriculum, students learn philanthropy's place in history, find charitable themes in literature and the arts, realize the importance of the nonprofit sector in maintaining a democratic society, and explore ways they can contribute to the betterment of their communities. The curriculum starts in kindergarten because even young children can understand the concepts of sharing time, talent and treasure. "At that age they can say 'stegosaurus,' so why not 'philanthropy'?" asks Agard. The high school curriculum explores careers in philanthropy. One in eight jobs in our economy, Agard points out, is in the nonprofit sector. "Students need to see philanthropy as a possible career."

Samples of the curriculum and all the classroom lessons are available on the Internet (see the Resources section). "We are modeling it in Michigan," says Agard, "but our intention is to go

The House That PRIDE Built

The Noble County Community Foundation in Ligonier, Indiana, provides volunteer docents who teach the county's third graders about philanthropy. The program is designed specifically for children in a sparsely populated rural community, says former Executive Director Nancy Plummer. The lessons use examples the kids can relate to, such as a farmer getting hurt and his friends banding together to harvest his crop. The foundation then gives each class $100 to donate to charity. "Some teachers don't want to be bothered, and the kids just send the whole amount to the Humane Society," Plummer says. "But other teachers help their students shop for ingredients, make dog biscuits, deliver them to the Humane Society and stay to help clean up." When the teachers get engaged in the lessons, the children do too.

The foundation fosters service by older kids by supporting a chapter of PRIDE, the Parents' Resource Institute for Drug Education program for middle and high school students. The chapter started with about 40 students in 1996. Now more than 600 participate, primarily in service projects after school with the help of adult leaders. In one project, older PRIDE students talk with fifth graders about the importance of abstaining from drugs, alcohol and tobacco.

One of the foundation's remarkable success stories was written by students who, while volunteering in a homeless shelter, became attached to a boy whose mother was a victim of domestic violence. The boy needed a kidney transplant but he had no health insurance. In three months, the PRIDE kids raised $100,000 to finance the life-saving transplant.

"These kids aren't content with little things," Plummer explains. They also built a Habitat for Humanity house with the guidance of a 70-year-old volunteer contractor and help from a few parents who worked with them occasionally. The builders, mostly middle school students, called it The House That PRIDE Built.

international. The Internet gives us international reach very quickly."

 TIP: Consider talking to your school administration about using this curriculum as part of your child's education. You might also approach local funding organizations about providing seed capital for teacher training to bring the K–12 project into your community's schools.

Help from Religious Institutions

All faiths embrace the tenet of serving others. Although the term philanthropy is not typically used, congregations teach the necessity of giving, sharing and "stewardship"—caring for humans, animals and the earth. Jewish tradition stresses that caring for others is a responsibility, not a choice. Children learn of mitzvot (good deeds) and tzedakah (charity). Muslim children are taught that giving is one of the five pillars of Islam.

After families, religious institutions exert the most influence on children's understanding of philanthropy. Studies show that teenagers are more likely to donate money to their congregation than to any other institution and that more of them become involved in volunteering through a religious institution than through school or other groups.

In addition to teaching philanthropic concepts during worship, some faiths involve young people in service through youth groups, retreats, summer camps and mission trips. Parochial school curricula typically include at least some mention of students' responsibility to society.

Connecting to Religious Holidays and Cultural Celebrations

Congregations often engage children in projects around holidays such as Thanksgiving, Passover, Christmas and Easter. African-American families who celebrate Kwanzaa share with their children the seven goals of the holiday, including ujima, which represents collective work and responsibility.

Many families use these occasions to collect canned goods or pack food baskets to make sure poor families have holiday meals. Some congregations sponsor holiday "gift shops" where members can donate money to charities in the name of those on their gift lists. One charity that's popular with children is The Heifer Project. Through this charity, children can pool money—sometimes their Sunday school offerings—to buy a gift of livestock, such as a cow that will provide milk for a family in a developing country.

Evan Mendelson, executive director of the Jewish Funders Network, says Jewish families use holidays such as Passover to teach philanthropy. She notes the Seder, for example, a family meal featuring special prayers and the telling of the Passover story. One Seder tradition is that a piece of matzah is hidden, and the child in the family who finds it gets a small gift. In some families the gift is a small amount of money that the child can donate to charity. Families who typically give a present to their child on each night of Hanukkah often require their child do some service for others during that week. Some Jewish families volunteer in hospitals and nursing homes on Christian holidays so Christian employees can have the day off to celebrate with their families.

Mendelson's organization wants Jewish day schools to use Michigan's K–12 Project, incorporating Jewish tradition and history. Much of the Jewish children's service education is now centered on 12- and 13-year-olds preparing for their bar or bat mitzvahs. Some young people are required to perform community service during the preparation period.

What Congregations Could Do Better

Gene Roehlkepartain, author of *Kids Have a Lot to Give: How Congregations Can Nurture Habits of Giving and Serving for the Common Good* (Search Institute, 1999), says congregations could do a lot more to teach children about giving. He is communications director for The Search Institute, a research organization that has conducted studies on several facets of children and philanthropy, including what faith communities are doing.

"Kids have more responsibility for their money, yet their giving is still relegated to a quarter in the offering plate that parents give them at the last minute," Roehlkepartain explains. He worries that advertisers and retailers have become the major influence on how children spend their considerable allowances. "They are developing habits of materialism that will last throughout their lives. Meanwhile, congregations aren't comfortable talking to kids directly about their responsibility to donate money."

He says one of the reasons is that adults aren't comfortable themselves about discussing money and giving, even in church. Some ministers often shy away from the subject, except to preach during the annual stewardship drive about the need to support the church's operating budget.

"For kids, that's not where they are. They need tangible things they can give to," such as mission projects, Roehlkepartain insists. "Historically, we've thought about kids as receivers, not givers," Roehlkepartain claims. "We do for them. We're afraid we'll scare kids away from religious institutions by imposing on them. But kids are trying to figure out who they are in the world and how they can make a difference, so engaging them in giving will actually retain them."

Evan Mendelson wants to revive some old traditions that encouraged giving. She remembers that her grandparents always had a tzedakah box where family members placed money to give to the poor. "Families today have gotten away from that tradition, but it's one place young children learned about giving."

Mission Trips

Participation in religious mission trips can encourage children to become more philanthropic. Some congregation members may ask why their church spends money to send kids on a trip to help needy people far away when plenty need help at home. Another criticism is that a one-shot service project doesn't allow participants to build a connection with the people they help. Research shows that ongoing projects that kids engage in regularly are more

---

Churches Should Emphasize Giving

Fred Smith is president of The Gathering, a fellowship of individuals, families and foundations that give to Christian ministries. He, too, worries that many churches are failing to teach youth to donate money.

"Someone needs to go to the Sunday school teachers," Smith suggests. "This is where I learned to give, not in the worship service. Teachers would feel more comfortable teaching this if parents urged them to. Those of us who have a relationship with the pastor should raise the issue. I teach a Sunday school class, and two out of four Sundays we talk about money and about creating the habit of giving. Most of the people who love giving learned the habit as a child."

Smith, who is also president of the Fourth Partner Foundation, believes children are generous but must have someone help them connect to groups that need their money. "If you ask them questions, you find out a lot of kids are spending money on gifts for other kids. They don't know about nonprofits." He also believes in celebrating giving. "When I see my kids give to something, I make a big deal of it and say, 'Is there anything I can do to help?'"

His daughters, aged 15 and 20, have often volunteered with him. He recalls one project in which they helped rehabilitate a hotel that had been a drug haven so it could be used for housing. "We cleaned up needles and lighters," he remembers. The experience made a big impression on the girls. His oldest daughter will spend part of her summer vacation from college working with disabled children at a hospital in Africa: "She'll come back with all sorts of ideas about giving."

---

effective. Will a mission have lasting value or be just an adventure for kids with little long-term impact?

Roehlkepartain acknowledges some legitimacy in such concerns, "but when I talk to people who do mission trips, they see a number of good results." The best mission programs are models for how to serve effectively, so adult youth advisers can learn how to improve their local community service programs.

"The adventure aspect also may draw in kids who wouldn't normally do service," Roehlkepartain points out. "Then they might have a life-changing experience, seeing living conditions they aren't normally exposed to in their sheltered lives, and continue serving when they go home."

Employers Can Help

Recognizing the value of service to their communities and their employees, a growing number of employers are creating corporate volunteer programs for families. By being allowed to include their kids, time-strapped parents become more likely to engage in community service.

A 1997 Conference Board survey found that 57 percent of corporations in the previous five years had begun encouraging family participation in corporate volunteer projects. One example is Target stores, which has succeeded in engaging the vast majority of its employees' families in corporate-sponsored volunteer work. The company's efforts were recognized by President Clinton in 1997 with the presentation of the President's Volunteer Award.

Foundations are supporting companies' efforts. The Family Matters program, the Points of Light initiative discussed earlier, has developed a model that connects agencies and volunteers with local businesses to create volunteer jobs and to recruit the volunteers.

 TIP: If you work for or own a business that doesn't sponsor volunteer opportunities, consider proposing such a program. Companies that support volunteering say it reaps payoffs in good community relations and greater employee loyalty. Small businesses can facilitate volunteerism by joining with others to promote a service project.

Youth Organizations

Youth groups such as 4-H, Camp Fire and scouts have proved to be among the most effective incubators of volunteerism.

The Girl Scouts, with a long history of fostering community service, recently created a philanthropy patch for members to earn. Unveiled during the 1999 White House Conference on Philanthropy, the "Strength in Sharing" patch requires girls to learn about philanthropists in their own families and communities, identify community needs and understand how their own time and money can make a difference. The youngest—Daisy Scouts (five- to six-year-olds)—can earn the patch by learning the meaning of philanthropy and how to identify examples of giving. Older scouts learn about careers in philanthropy and human service. Those between the ages of 14 and 17 design and manage service projects and interact with local and national foundations.

Another organization that stresses community service is Jack and Jill of America, a 60-year-old organization dedicated to improving the quality of life for children, particularly African Americans. Led by mothers and with support from fathers, the children are grouped by age: 2–5, 6–8, 9–12 and teenagers. Each is required to volunteer in the community.

Giving Kids a Pat on the Back

Children who render outstanding community service deserve praise. When they're young, a kind word from a parent or another adult may be enough. Older kids will appreciate validation from the larger community.

For example, organizations can nominate volunteers aged 5 to 25 for the President's Student Service Awards. Modeled after the President's Physical Fitness Awards, the program bestows a gold pin, certificate and letter from the president on young people who perform at least 100 hours of service in a 12-month period. Silver Awards are given to children 5 to 14 who serve 50 hours in a year. If you know a deserving child, see the Resources section for

---

story

Safety on Site

Eileen Cackowski recalls a Habitat for Humanity project that was reluctant to have children on site because of the dangers posed by hammers, saws and other potentially hazardous tools. One dad said, "I'm not going to spend another Saturday away from my kids." Another adult proposed a safer activity at the Habitat site. He gathered the children of volunteers in a corner of the yard and helped them build a bird house. Then, with his supervision, the kids painted the fence around the property and planted flowers. Among the volunteers were the children of the family for whom the house was being built. "Everyone can give," Cackowski remarks. "And we forget that sometimes."

---

information on nominations. Publicity can expand public support for the cause your children support, as well as give them a pat on the back.

 TIP: Don't hesitate to contact the media when you know of a youth-led project that deserves publicity. They love good-news, human-interest stories.

When Agencies Are Reluctant to Use Young Volunteers

Agencies used to dealing with adults may not welcome children. They worry about liability and the extra supervision required. Some are willing to accept children when they are joined by their parents.

Cackowski asks a pointed question of agencies that say they have no jobs that children and adults can do together: "Do you want volunteers in ten years? Kids who volunteer become adults who volunteer." She helps nonprofit organizations divide jobs into parts, including some that are safe for children, and teaches risk management. Take, for example, a food pantry that stores items on high shelves. Children shouldn't be allowed to climb on ladders, but older ones might be able to manage extension poles to reach the top shelves. Younger ones could pack items into boxes.

Agencies often worry that a group of young volunteers may be inclined to "fool around and have a good time rather than complete a task," observes Becky Wagner, director of an interfaith agency serving the poor. "Usually, that happens if the task assigned

---

story

United Way Offers Adventures

United Way executive Deborah Fenton of Springfield, Massachusetts, takes lots of calls from teachers and youth group leaders who want to find volunteer projects for their charges. Putting her experience as a preschool teacher to work, Fenton created United Way Adventurers. She developed 45 cards listing projects that children could do to help local agencies. There are 15 projects in each of three categories—people, animals and the environment. She encourages youth leaders to narrow the selection and let the children choose which activities to take on.

She linked an elementary school with a program delivering meals to homebound elderly, for example. The children wrote seasonal greetings that were delivered with the meals, and the seniors wrote back. "It didn't cost the teacher anything and didn't take the children away from school," Fenton notes. A kindergarten class made a piñata and delivered it to children at the Shriners hospital. And junior high school students made adaptive toys for children with disabilities. In the process they learned to appreciate how such children can overcome their physical challenges.

Fenton's experience shows that many projects can be accomplished by younger children or expanded to fit the abilities of older ones. Participants in this program earn a United Way Adventurers appreciation certificate and the satisfaction of helping others.

is so menial that it's hard for the kids to see the value at the other end of it."

Wagner's organization mitigates that risk by making sure its young volunteers have meaningful work. She cites the example of some high school students who signed on to shop for school supplies and book bags for needy children. After the purchasing and sorting were done, the students decided they wanted to distribute the supplies personally to the recipients. They wrote thank-you letters to donors and a lead article for the agency's newsletter. "The students basically took over the project and owned it," Wagner says.

 TIP: Timing is everything. Agencies serving the poor may be inundated with volunteer offers at Thanksgiving and Christmas but get little interest at other times of the year. It's a good bet that your local food pantry could use your help more in June than December. And it's often easier for students to volunteer during summer vacation.

---

story

Kids Helping Kids

Daniela Young, 14, who helped distribute school supplies at the Community Ministry of Montgomery County, Maryland, wrote in its newsletter that "looking into the eyes of each child warmed my heart. Whenever I went back to the center, I couldn't wait to get started. I felt joy from doing this good deed, but sad when I saw children having to go through the experience of a complete stranger taking care of their school preparation."

Daniela also wrote that seeing people in need "made me realize that these people are no different from you and me. The thought that I was somehow 'better' than these people made me sick to my stomach. I am certain that I will never look at things the same way ever again. I will see people with an open mind and an open heart."

---

story

A Club That's 10,000 Students Strong

It could be the biggest youth volunteer organization in the country, with 10,000 teens enrolled. Members of the ManaTEEN Club in Manatee County, Florida, give more than a million hours of service a year. One of the reasons the program attracts so many kids is that Adraine La Roza, the county's executive director of volunteer services who oversees the program, takes them seriously and gives them responsibility.

"She doesn't care if they are 'A' students or 'D' students or popular or not," says Eileen Cackowski. "Her only expectation is that they will serve." La Roza doesn't micromanage or make the plans. She lets the kids take charge. "They love it because they are understood and they aren't treated like children," Cackowski observes. "We grown-ups often are afraid to step away and allow projects to happen."

CHAPTER FOUR

Money 101:
Teaching Kids Money
Management and Giving

How can we expect our children to know and experience
the joy of giving, unless we teach them that the greater
pleasure in life lies in the art of giving rather than receiving?

—JAMES CASH (J. C.) PENNEY

Kids today have more cash than any previous generation. By some estimates, teens alone spent a record $141 billion in 1999, up from $122 billion in 1997. They also have considerable influence on their parents' spending decisions. This financial clout has not been lost on marketers. They are bypassing parents to pitch hard-sell messages to kids as young as preschool age. Yet many of these children who are being asked to part with their money have never learned the basics of how to make financial choices. And the marketers typically aren't promoting charitable donations.

That's why you have to start your children's financial education early—as soon as they begin to ask about money. If you get a jump on the influence of Madison Avenue, your child will be more likely to make wise spending decisions, including sharing with others. Experts say that with young children, the goal should be establishing the habit of giving, regardless of which group kids give their money to, or why. Over time, you can teach a child how to think more strategically about doing the most good.

 TIP: For interesting dinner table conversation, ask your kids what messages they receive about money from television, school, friends, family and other sources. You might be surprised to hear what they are absorbing, especially from the media. And to counter the barrage of kid-targeted advertising, talk about the commercials when you watch TV together, pointing out that products don't always live up to their hype.

Early Lessons about Money and Giving

If you offer a kindergartner a dime and a nickel and tell him to pick one, he's likely to choose the nickel. It's bigger, he figures, so it must be worth more. Money is an abstract concept to children. Whether it's the six-year-old trying to distinguish between a one-dollar bill and five-dollar bill or the 13-year-old who has no savings because she spends her allowance as soon as she gets it, handling money is complex. Where it comes from is confusing too. When preschoolers see you take crisp bills from an ATM, they don't realize you had to make a deposit earlier.

Helping your children sort it out is a process that should start when they are very young and continue through their teenage years. Along the way, you'll impart your family's values about how to use resources and how to share with others. Even children whose parents never discuss money with them will absorb some lessons from the example their parents set by their actions—though the lessons may not be exactly what these parents want to teach.

Having "The Talk"

It's one thing to explain how an ATM works and quite another to delve into your family's values about money. In some families, talking about money is more taboo than discussing sex. Money has emotional connotations, no matter how much of it you had growing up. Parents are often uncomfortable talking about

---

activity

Personal Values about Money and Giving

Before parents can convey their values about money and philanthropy to their children, they need to examine just what their own values are. Knowing how you feel about using money and about contributing some of it to causes you feel passionate about will help you guide your children. Try this activity from the book *Inspired Philanthropy* (Chardon Press, 1998) by Tracy Gary and Melissa Kohner (used with permission).

Indicators of Your Values

In whatever way works best for you—free writing, quiet thought or a conversation with a friend—explore one or more of the following questions that you find interesting. Write your answers below.

- What experiences and people have been key in shaping your core values and passions?
- What do you notice about your values when you consider your choices, such as life directions, career, free time, lifestyle, donations and spending?
- When you hear of world events or witness an injustice, what moves you most? With what have you been most troubled? Most delighted?

After you've answered these questions, compare your values with how you actually use money in your daily life. Does your lifestyle reflect those values? Are the organizations you support the ones with missions reflecting your passions? Are changes in order? When you've reflected on this, use this information to help you articulate your values to your children.

---

finances with their children. But that doesn't stop children from asking difficult questions.

Sex educators say that parents should not just explain the facts of life to their kids but also impart their own values about sexuality, because children equipped with such knowledge are more likely to make wise decisions. The same is true when the subject is money.

"How Much Money Do We Make?"

Many people feel their financial status should remain private. But openness about the family's finances, at least to some degree, makes children better able to manage money and more likely to become givers as opposed to materialists.

Janet Bodnar, executive editor of *Kiplinger's Personal Finance* magazine, recommends that parents answer their child's question "How much money do we make?" by saying, "More than some families but not as much as others." She thinks parents are entitled to their privacy and may not want the figure blabbed on the playground. Besides, the amount probably won't be meaningful to younger children, to whom any annual salary will seem enormous. By the time children enter their teenage years, they can be given a general idea of the family's income, Bodnar says, "but you don't have to show them your net worth." The subject might come up in a discussion of how expensive a college your family can afford.

What if your kids ask: "Are we rich?" Bodnar advises replying that your family has enough to buy what it needs and have some left over to share. Remember, too, that children need to hear that a rich life doesn't require lots of money and that self-worth isn't measured by bank account balances. That's also a good time to remind kids not to brag to others about how much money the family has.

When children wonder why their parents don't buy something the kids want, Bodnar suggests explaining that "we can afford it but we choose to do other things with our money." Parents can say they are saving for their children's education or their own retirement or to give to charity, for example. Kids also need to understand that no matter how much a family earns, a portion of its income must pay for the mortgage, utilities, food, clothes and other family expenses.

Philanthropic Values Are Not Just for the Wealthy

Lessons about money and giving are important for all children, regardless of their family's income, and philanthropy does not imply great wealth. Tracy Gary is coauthor of *Inspired Philanthropy* and spent 14 years as director of Resourceful Women, a nonprofit organization she started in her early 30s. Gary points out that poorer families—those making less than $10,000—donate 4 percent of their income to charity, whereas median-income Americans donate only about 2 percent. The poor families "see how giving works," she says. They know that a spirit of generosity can sustain the community.

John Romo of New York City is of Mexican descent and was once a teacher in a low-income Latino community in Southern California. "I was amazed by the comments made by really poor parents and kids about making sure that they shared what they had," Romo recalls from his time in that community. "I remember giving a writing assignment to a class of kids who had very recently immigrated from Mexico, fifth and sixth graders, asking them what they would do if they were suddenly given $1,000. The first thing most of the kids wrote is that they would give some of it to the poor—and most of these kids were really poor themselves."

Romo notes that in Mexican culture, "helping others is tied to a responsibility not to forget one's roots. My grandmother was great at reminding us about our responsibilities. She would often take me aside and tell me how proud she was that I had gone to college and that I was doing well. She'd follow this, however, with the stern admonition: 'Don't ever forget where you came from and the people who are still back there.'"

Wealthy parents are not always so clear about the messages they pass on to the next generation. "From the moment they have a child, wealthy parents worry their children will suffer from having inherited money. But they don't pay attention to how they are modeling" wise use of resources, says Gary. "There's nothing that says that just because you have made money, your children are

---

activity

Messages about Money Values

(Adapted from a chart by Joan DiFuria of the Money, Meaning and Choices Institute. Used with permission.)

Parents face difficult choices in handling their wealth. Some of these are listed below. Each family must decide where it stands. Go down the list and mark which view you hold and the most important values for your family:

Allowances should be tied to chores.	Chores should be independent of the allowance.
My children should inherit everything I have.	My children should not get everything.
I believe money can be a motivator to my children.	I believe money gets in the way of motivation.
I want to encourage my children to have friends of different social classes.	I believe my children will be more comfortable staying among children of their own social class.
The inheritance I leave my child will have strings attached.	My child may use her inheritance as she wishes.
I am comfortable giving my children regular financial gifts during my lifetime.	I will pass my money to my children after my death.

---

entitled to an automatic benefit," Bodnar adds. As you consider your teenager's clothing budget, for example, "think what a kid reasonably needs, not what you can afford." Gary also notes that many wealthy families live in suburbs where they have little contact with a diverse population or with people who are poor. So wealthy parents need to talk to children about their world view, their economic level and what their responsibility is to the wider community.

Setting Boundaries in Giving

Although you don't want your children to be greedy, you also don't want them to give away everything they have. Some kids give money or gifts to other children so they'll be liked. Others want to give a handout to every homeless person they see—and they wonder why their parents don't too. "Explain to your children that the family has certain expenses, such as food and clothing and the light bill," Bodnar suggests. "Say, 'If we gave all our money away, we couldn't run our household, and then we would need help too.'"

Joan Indursky DiFuria, cofounder of Money, Meaning and Choices Institute, a San Francisco consulting organization, notes that children need help understanding boundaries. Just because a friend can't afford to take a trip with them doesn't mean they should pay for their friend's trip. Instead, they can learn to appreciate differences in families and understand that friendship should be based on bonds that are independent of family income.

As for giving to every homeless person, parents can explain that the family doesn't have enough to meet everyone's needs. There are other ways the child can help. Brainstorm with him about alternatives, such as collecting canned goods for the local soup kitchen. Tell your children that, because they can't give to every charity that asks, there are ways to choose which ones they want to support, such as requesting more information or visiting it. Offer to help them do research or make a site visit. Initially, kids may be most effective if they give to groups with which they already are familiar; for example, donating a book to the school library or buying food for their congregation's baskets for the needy.

Starting an Allowance

Children can learn about generosity if parents give them funds with which to make donations. But they'll learn even more when they've got some money of their own. Then they can decide whether to spend their money only on themselves or give a portion to charity.

Somewhere around first grade, children begin learning about money at school—simple lessons such as ten dimes equal a dollar. Experts say that's a good time to start giving kids an allowance. DiFuria urges clients to give allowances to teach their children the skills they'll need to become financially competent adults. "I tell them to let the kids make little blunders now so they'll learn before they have to make crucial fiscal decisions."

How Much Should the Allowance Be?

Talking with other parents who have children in the same age group as yours can give you a picture of what typical allowances are in your community. The allowance should reflect your child's age and the financial responsibility you tie to the allowance. "For

---

statistics

Allowances in the United States

The 1997 Ohio State University study found that half of all teenagers get an allowance, typically about $50 a week. Teens from high-income families are more likely to receive allowances than teens in families with more modest incomes and, not surprisingly, the amount they receive is generally higher too. For teenagers from families with annual household incomes of at least $100,000, the average allowance was $175 a week. Teenagers in households making between $20,000 and $30,000 received an average of $19 a week.

example," Bodnar suggests, "a first grader can be told that his allowance has to cover collectibles," such as stickers or baseball cards. Or you could tell your child he'll have to pay for his own treats from the ice cream truck, snacks from vending machines or games at the video arcade. Once you determine what your child will be responsible for (including charitable giving), you can set the allowance level that you think is reasonable.

As your children grow older, you can increase the amount and add to what they are expected to pay for, such as movies or clothes. DiFuria urges clients to "set rules and stick by them. Let the kid blow all his money on one video game and don't bail him out. Otherwise, you take away the power of the lesson." Bodnar agrees that a parent shouldn't buy things for the children that their allowances are supposed to cover. Help them learn to live within their budgets.

Most experts say every child should be required to do chores as part of his or her responsibility to the family, not to earn an allowance. If your children do not complete their chores, you can impose such sanctions as loss of TV privileges. If you rely on the allowance to enforce performance of chores, a child who doesn't care about money can opt not to help around the house and therefore not be a contributing member of the family. If kids want to earn extra money, you can pay them for jobs they offer to do beyond their regular chores.

Allowances and Benevolent Giving

Parents often wonder if it's okay to require that some of the allowance be used for charitable giving. Bodnar, who also writes a nationally syndicated column on kids and money called "Dr. Tightwad," thinks it's fine for parents to mandate that a child donate part to charity. "It's okay to use the allowance to instill the values you want to convey," she says. DiFuria agrees. She thinks giving an allowance without structure can cause harm by teaching the wrong lessons. She recommends requiring a minimum of 10 percent go to charity, with other portions set aside for spending and saving. But DiFuria suggests waiting until kids are older to add a fourth money lesson—investment. Some parents eventually require a portion be set aside as long-term savings for such expenses as college tuition.

Kim McGuire, program director for the Community Foundation of Western North Carolina, divides her nine-year-old daughter's $6 allowance into thirds: for spending, for savings and for giving. Some families call this the "three jar" system, because their kids use three labeled jars to keep the amounts separated. If that's your plan, Bodnar suggests giving the child an allowance easily divisible by three, such as $3 or $9, as McGuire does. If your child's allowance doesn't fit that model, then specify a certain amount—say, $1—that should go to charity. Bodnar cautions parents to keep the allowance system simple; otherwise, parents won't stick to it and the child won't learn much about managing money.

 TIP: A 1997 survey by researchers at Ohio State University found that U.S. teenagers (12- to 18-year-olds) are given a total of $1.05 billion each week in allowances. If teenagers donated just 10 percent to charity, the impact would be staggering!

Next Steps in Money Management

As children grow up and their allowance or job income rises, their parents need to gradually introduce them to sound ways of managing their money. Tracy Gary says many low- and middle-income parents teach their kids financial skills at a much earlier age than wealthy parents tend to do. For example, many lower-income shoppers teach their children what things are worth and how to negotiate. But whether rich or poor, adults should teach kids life skills and introduce them to the tools they will need for good stewardship of their resources.

Not all young people will find money management an interesting topic. Take a cue from your children about the pace at which they want to learn. Otherwise, you'll risk turning them off to the whole subject. And don't make assumptions about your daughters' level of interest. A 1998 Harris poll of ninth through eleventh

Buried Treasure

Eileen Growald started giving her two sons allowances around the age of six, encouraging them to save a third, spend a third and give a third. She and her husband also talked freely with their children about the causes to which they gave money. The trouble was, their oldest son seldom parted with any of his money. "He didn't even buy candy," Growald recalled. When he was ten and was receiving $10 a week, "we insisted that he spend $2 a week," so he'd have the experience of making choices about how to spend money. The plan backfired when, fearing his parents were going to make him part with his hoard, he buried it in the back yard.

Now that he's 14, he's still cautious about using his money. But he's finding ways to be philanthropic, sometimes without using his own funds. Recently, he discovered two Web sites with sponsors that will send donations—one to feed the hungry and the other to preserve rain forests—every time a visitor clicks on one of the sites. He sent a message to his parents, other relatives and friends, telling them about the sites and urging them to visit often. He set his own computer to automatically click on the rain forest site whenever he opens his e-mail program. He also enthusiastically performs community service through his school, working with kindergarten students as a mentor.

"Someday, he'll feel good about giving his own money, but right now he has to find his own way," Growald says. "I'm glad we didn't push him harder. It's so important to meet children at their own level while still being clear about the meaning that giving has for you personally." There's danger in forcing children to give or telling them what to support, Growald warns. If they are not giving "with a full heart," there's little joy in it and parents' well-intentioned efforts may not encourage lifelong philanthropy.

graders found girls and boys equally interested in money and finance. The girls just lagged in knowledge and confidence. Experts say girls' reluctance to become stock market players probably stems from society's tendency to reward boys for risk-taking more than girls.

Learning about Bank Accounts

When your kids are young, giving them a see-through piggy bank can allow them to visualize how their money accumulates. But as children get older and outgrow their piggy banks, consider helping them open a bank account. Your bank may offer accounts for minors, but make sure you know about any minimum balance requirements or service charges before letting your child sign up. Monthly fees could eat up all the interest and even the principal if your child's account is small. It may be easier to act as the bank yourself.

When Eileen Growald of Shelburne, Vermont, began giving her two sons allowances, she also gave them small ledgers and taught them how to record debits and credits. Other parents keep their child's bank record in the home computer, using a financial program to calculate monthly interest on the balance so the child learns that saving money earns a return. If you use this approach, consider offering a generous rate of interest—say, 10 percent—if your child's allowance is small. Otherwise, the interest won't add up to much and the child won't be as motivated to save.

You might also make your middle or high schooler responsible for balancing the family checkbook, for example, or for writing some of the checks to your family's favorite charities. Or consider having her write checks to pay your utility bills. It might be eye-opening for her to see how high your long-distance telephone bills are, for example, especially if she contributes to those expenses. Or try challenging your kids to become the power police. They can help lower your electric bill by turning off the lights or televisions when not in use. As an incentive for their diligence, tell them they can have the savings if your next bill is lower.

 TIP: Young Americans Bank of Denver is the first and only bank specifically for kids. The average age of its savings account holders is nine and their average balance is $534. The bank provides other financial services too, including checking accounts, ATM cards, loans and certificates of deposit—all available by mail. Check it out at **www.theyoungamericans.org** or write: Young Americans Bank, 311 Steele Street, Denver, CO 80206. Phone 303/321-2265.

Kids and the Stock Market

Children who have an interest-bearing bank account (or a parent who acts as the bank and pays interest) have already learned a bit about investments. Some adolescents take investing to the next level and try the stock market. Some belong to school investment clubs through which they play the market, though not with real money. Some parents buy their children a few shares in a company the child recognizes—Disney, McDonald's and the like. As your child learns to make his money grow, you can also point out how much more he'll have available for giving as well as for spending.

---

story

Taking Stock

Gita Drury's mother wanted her to learn both how to manage money and how to be philanthropic with it. "When I was about 16, I went to our financial manager and stockbroker, who started my financial literacy education," Drury says. "She wanted me to learn about the stock market." Drury picked two stocks "connected with my teenage life," the Gap and the BodyShop. That was ten years ago and both proved very wise investments. But she admits that she was not very interested in following her investments. Her typical teenage day didn't include checking stock quotes. The payoff came later. Now in her 20s, Drury used her investments to join with four other young donors in starting the Active Element Foundation, which supports youth activists across the country.

---

story

Tracy Gary's Financial Education

When Tracy Gary was young, her parents used several devices to teach her about giving. By age 14, they gave her $100 a year to put in a "giving account" from which she could make grants. "If we volunteered more than five hours a week during the summer, we got incentive gifts to add to our giving account. If I gave my own money [from her allowance] it was matched. They taught us a system. If we were interested in pandas, we kept files on them. We were to learn about issues we cared about and then connect the dots." In return for the giving accounts, Gary's parents made one request. "They asked me to keep a record and, at the end of the year, 'share the one favorite grant you made and what you learned.'"

 TIP: Stein Roe has a Young Investor Fund with low minimum requirements. You can set up a custodial account for your child for as little as $100 if you agree to add $50 a month to the fund. Or you can make a $1,000 investment with no additional investments required. The bonus is that kids with accounts in the fund receive lots of educational material to help them learn about money. Check it out at **www.steinroe.com** or call 800/338-2550. Also check the Resources section of this book for a list of money management seminars and camps for children.

CHAPTER FIVE

Not Just Writing a Check: Giving Money Effectively

Tell me and I'll forget. Show me and I may not remember.
Involve me and I'll understand.

—NATIVE AMERICAN PROVERB

Children are capable of more than adults sometimes give them credit for. After you've worked with them on managing money, they can learn to give it away effectively. Start with simple concepts and progress from there, gradually giving them more freedom to make decisions.

Even kindergartners can express their views about which causes to support. As they grow older, you can help your children learn to choose wisely among worthy causes, to research the services provided by possible recipients of grants, to evaluate how effective the grantees are and to determine how to allocate the money—small donations to many organizations or large grants to a few.

The Dinner Table Foundation

Here's a simplified version of a grantmaking foundation. Gather the family around the dining room table, bring along information on the various requests you've received for donations and whatever amount—large or small—that is set aside in the family's budget for benevolent giving. Then let your children have a say in which organizations will receive the family's donations. Those who've tried it say it's a powerful way to expose even very young children to the importance of sharing with others and to help them learn how to go about it. Just make sure, if your children are young, to keep the discussion simple and the meeting short.

Parents can present the options for children to pick from. Or, if the kids are old enough, they can bring their own ideas. At an initial meeting, the children can brainstorm about their interests—animals, the environment or sports, for example. Then help them research specific groups that work in those areas. For example, a child might consider helping the local animal shelter, a group that's cleaning up a nearby river or a soccer team that provides scholarships to kids who can't afford registration fees or equipment. If you want to take the research to the next level, you can even go on family field trips (kid terminology for site visits) to see how some local charities deliver their services. Or volunteer in one that your dinner table foundation is considering supporting.

Armed with their research findings, the children return to the table for the grantmaking meeting in which the family decides how many grants to make and in what amounts. The level of their involvement—and their attention span—depends, of course, on the children's ages. Don't wait a year between meetings. The subject will stay fresh with the children if the dinner table foundation makes allocations three or four times a year. Some families let each child designate a portion of the funds to his own favorite charities. Others decide together as a family with a majority-rules vote. Some combine both approaches.

Gene Roehlkepartain's family has been doing this for several years, beginning when his children were three and nine. "At the end of the year, we put all the solicitations on the table and let the kids pick some," Roehlkepartain explains. His younger child always chose the ones that helped animals. Although that wasn't high on the parents' list of giving preferences, they let the chil-

activity

Holding a Dinner Table Foundation Meeting

What you'll need: an easel or pad of newsprint, markers, memo pads and pencils for each family member; mailings requesting donations; play money (optional).

1. Decide in advance of the meeting what amount your family will give to charity.

2. If your children are young, you should also predetermine how funding decisions will be made (e.g., each family member picks his or her own charities, the family votes on them as a group, or a combination of the two methods). If your children are older, they may want to participate in devising the plan.

3. Set the time and place for the family meeting. At that time, turn off the TV, let the answering machine catch your phone calls and take other steps as necessary to ensure you aren't interrupted by distractions.

4. On the top of the easel or large pad, post the amount of money you plan to have the family allocate to charity.

5. Explain how the decisions will be made.

6. List the preferences of each family member on the pad.

7. Use the play money to help the kids visualize how the money could be divided among the chosen charities.

8. Vote on which organizations to fund and in what amounts.

9. Let the kids help you write the checks.

Note: When your children are very young, keep the meeting brief (20 minutes for kindergartners) and limit the choice of charities to three or four that are likely to appeal to them (e.g., the local animal shelter). Don't focus on the amounts to be given until they are old enough to understand money.

dren have their say. Over time, their interests changed. "Last year, he chose things that were in aid of children's issues," Roehlkepartain recalls. He believes that regardless of which charities the children pick, the exercise is valuable. "My hope is that, over time, as he internalizes positive values, that will be reflected in his giving," Roehlkepartain says of his younger child.

 TIP: One place to research national charities is through the Wise Giving Alliance (**www.give.org**), formerly a program of the National Charities Information Bureau. Also look at **www.guidestar.org**, which has information on more than 60,000 nonprofit organizations.

Matching What Kids Give

Some families give their children funds to make donations. That way, children have a larger amount of money to work with than would be possible from saving a portion of their allowance. Other families supplement the grants their children make from their own funds.

Laura Kind McKenna, a managing trustee of the Patricia Kind Family Foundation, has four children, ranging in age from 11 to 18. "I've always said, 'Tell me what you want to give to and I'll match it,'" she explains. Sometimes she'll give more than a dollar-for-dollar match, "but there's always a sense of it coming partly from their own money." She's happy to reward effort too, such as sponsoring her children's participation in the American Cancer Society's Relay for Life, the Philadelphia AIDS Walk, and Walk for Hunger.

Fred Smith of both The Gathering and The Fourth Partner Foundation is a proponent of matching children's giving. He cautions parents against just handing their kids money to use for their church offerings or other donations without expecting them to give money of their own.

Connecting Children with Grantees

Especially when they begin, children are inclined to give to familiar organizations, such as their school or the YMCA where they play sports. Eventually, however, they'll probably want to expand their reach and give to organizations about which they have no firsthand knowledge. While it's certainly okay if they want to help save rain forests in South America, they'll learn to be more effective givers if they can see the impact of their money whenever possible. Many agencies are willing to have families tour their

---

story

Giving Locally vs. Giving Globally

When Gita Drury was 15, her mom started giving her $2,000 a year to donate to the organizations of her choice. "At the time, I was interested in things having to do with animals," Drury recalls. She gave to organizations such as Greenpeace, the World Wildlife Fund and People for the Ethical Treatment of Animals. "The funny thing about it was that once I became a high-level donor, $500 to $1,000, I started getting invited to black-tie events. They didn't realize they were inviting a 15-year-old to buy a table."

The exercise in grantmaking didn't last long because she felt disconnected from the organizations she was funding. By the time she was 18, her mother stopped giving her the money because Drury hadn't spent all the funds she'd already received. "All the things I funded were national organizations that sent mail solicitations. I wasn't involved locally. And I didn't see how my contribution was making that much difference. I lost interest."

It was during and after college, when she participated in social justice groups, that she found her grantmaking niche. "Now I'm less interested in funding big national organizations when there are so many grassroots organizations where $1,000 will make a huge difference."

The Student Who Dreamed of Helping Kosovo Refugees

With a mother who was always fundraising and volunteering for one good cause or another, Hiliary Critchley Plioplys of Washington, DC, learned the ropes from a very young age. During her junior year of high school, she and friend Elizabeth Schroth formed a group called People for Peace. The organization's mission statement said it was "a student-run group which educates young people about key societal issues and mobilizes them to act on that awareness."

People for Peace started with small projects. They circulated petitions, invited guest speakers and gathered information about community service options during summer break. They held a grilled cheese sandwich sale at school to raise money—"We wanted to do something different than a bake sale."

But then the group found a more challenging project. Their concern for Kosovo refugees led them to War Child, an international relief agency. War Child needed trucks to ship supplies to refugees. The girls learned a truck could be rented for $5,500. "It was a huge goal but we decided to go for it."

They blanketed their Catholic girls school with publicity about their cause and latched onto another unusual fundraising idea—Dress Down Day. The girls convinced their school administrator to let students skip wearing uniforms for one day if they paid $2 for the privilege. Most students donated far more to the cause. A kindergartner gave the proceeds from her mini-fundraiser—a lemonade stand. Others contributed their allowances and solicited generous donations from their parents. Alumnae who were holding a meeting in Washington added to the total. At the end of their fundraiser, People for

Peace had collected $16,700, more than enough for three trucks!

People for Peace's huge success netted them publicity, an award from the National Society of Fund Raising Executives and an invitation to speak at the association's national conference on philanthropy in spring 2000. Plioplys represented the group at the conference, speaking on a panel about women philanthropists. On the platform with her was Doris Bryant, founder of the Sunshine Lady Foundation. Through the foundation, Bryant chooses promising philanthropists, whom she calls Sunbeams. She lets them donate, through her foundation, to worthy groups or individuals. At the conference, Bryant invited Plioplys to be a Sunbeam. Plioplys now has $10,000 per year to use for advancing education, well-being and new life choices for disadvantaged people. She's still deciding what to fund.

On April 15, 2000, People for Peace once again made the news. The group received grants from Youth Service America and the Maryland lieutenant governor's office that helped them put on an event to promote National Youth Service Day. The girls organized a benefit concert at Washington's Kennedy Center that featured folk singer and activist Peter Yarrow of Peter, Paul and Mary, and speakers who emphasized the good things youth are accomplishing.

"We wanted to alter the vision the media have about youth today, which is so focused on youth violence," Plioplys says. "We spread the message that kids are doing good things and that they can make a huge difference in their communities. Our power should not be underestimated."

facilities. They know that a family who gets hooked on their program could be givers for many years to come.

Philanthropy consultant Tracy Gary reminds parents that Internet-savvy children can find ideas and information about worthy causes on-line and even make donations there. If they want to help pandas, for example, they can learn about the need to preserve panda habitats in China. But she advises parents to remind their children that "a virtual relationship isn't the same" as giving to animals at the local zoo.

Even young children can learn to evaluate organizations. Virginia Hubbell, a California philanthropy consultant, has worked with kids as young as four, helping them learn about organizations such as wildlife rescue centers and taking them on site visits. "They need to see the wounded birds," she says. And to make grant proposals digestible to young grantmakers, Hubbell puts them in child terms. Her daughter, at the age of eight, summarized proposals for the children of Hubbell's clients. "I had her do a letter that said 'you might think about this' and explained what the program was about—in an eight-year-old's voice."

Raising Money to Make Grants

Donating money has more meaning to children if they also have the satisfaction—and fun—of raising it through their hard work and creativity. And they can learn valuable skills in the process. Kids who organize a yard sale to help a Boys and Girls Club, for example, have to practice teamwork, handle publicity, price the merchandise, arrange displays, negotiate with customers, make change and add up the proceeds. (And their parents even get their closets cleaned out!)

Introducing Your Children to Grantmaking through Your Community Foundation

Some families use a donor-advised fund at their community foundation to help their children learn about grantmaking. There are more than 500 of these foundations across the country.

There are advantages to going through a community foundation rather than just writing checks yourself. The staff invests the money for you, recommends worthy projects for funding and handles administrative tasks such as check writing. Plus, your money is pooled with that of others to make a bigger impact in your local community. This approach also has tax advantages. Your family's money can be put into the foundation's general fund or can be held in a donor-advised fund that allows you to choose the organizations to be funded. The latter option gives families an opportunity to work with their children to make funding decisions.

Be aware that with a donor-advised fund, the gift to the community foundation is permanent, and final authority for grants and investments rests with the community foundation's board. The board technically has the power to override any recommendation the donor offers, but in practice this rarely happens. Nevertheless, donors who care about retaining full control might wish to pursue a different giving option.

Heather Larkin Eason, executive director of the Arkansas Community Foundation, finds that a growing number of families want to use this vehicle. Her foundation is typical in that it requires a $10,000 minimum to endow a donor-advised fund. She allows people to build up to that amount over three years or so. Once it reaches the minimum, the family can make grants from the interest. Her foundation has other options for people who want to put money—say $1,000—in a nonpermanent fund and spend it all in one year, with the foundation handling administrative work. But in that case, there is no endowment that can generate funds for future use by the family.

Some parents set up a donor-advised fund in which they work together with their children on grantmaking decisions. Other times, funds are created specifically for a child, siblings or even cousins. The foundation staff supplies the children with information on possible projects to fund and offers advice as needed. The idea is to give the children some independence from their adult relatives as they delve more deeply into grantmaking.

Sometimes grandparents are the ones using this vehicle. Making grants in collaboration with a grandchild can strengthen the

Grandchildren Funds

Mark Hollis' philanthropic education began at an early age when he was expected to tithe a penny to his church from his weekly ten-cent allowance. Later, when the family foundation his parents set up was going out of existence, he put his share into a donor-advised fund in the Community Foundation of Lakeland (Florida). Every year, six of his nine grandchildren—aged 7 through 19—get to suggest a charity to receive a $500 donation.

When the process began in 2000, 11-year-old grandson Clay chose Lighthouse Ministries, a shelter for homeless men that he'd visited with his Cub Scout troop to deliver donations of toiletries. Nine-year-old Jill selected a Girl Scout camp she's attended. In a letter to her grandparents explaining her reasoning, Jill wrote that her Brownie troop had gone there. "We had to make our own meals and pump water from a well. It was a good experience for us. . . . The money could be used for scholarships for girls who can't afford to go to the summer camp."

Originally, Hollis planned to let the grandchildren participate when they became teenagers. His children convinced him to include the younger grandchildren as well, promising to work with those who needed extra help. "What has surprised me is their level of understanding of philanthropy and how early they can catch on to this concept," Hollis says. He adds that the lesson "doesn't take a lot of money. For a ten-year-old, $500 is an enormous amount."

Georgia Welles of Bowling Green, Ohio, created the Granny Fund for her 14 grandchildren in 1998. It's actually five donor-advised funds at community foundations in the cities where her grandchildren reside. She put $25,000 in each fund and told her grandchildren they would have the responsibility of recommending where the interest would go. "It's up to them to choose whether to pool their funds with their siblings or make individual decisions," she explains.

Although she worried that the foundations wouldn't want to spend much time administering such small funds, she found the reception at each foundation to be very positive. She already had a long association as a donor to the Toledo Community Foundation—her son is the current board chair—but all five of the foundations have been very willing to provide staff support to the grandchildren as they learn about grantmaking firsthand.

In Boulder, Colorado, where three of the grandchildren grew up, the siblings meet at home during Christmas break to decide how to disburse their funds. The first year, the siblings toured an AIDS facility where one of them had volunteered, according to Lindsey Eklund, program officer for the Boulder foundation. "They asked wonderful questions," Eklund remembers. "That's where they decided to allocate their money, about $1,000." In 1999 they accepted the recommendation of their youngest sibling and gave a grant to the Humane Society. "We enjoy the chance to work with kids," Eklund adds, "because so rarely do you get the option of hearing what's on kids' minds."

Welles has been pleased with the results. "I feel it's empowering for them and instructional. One thing I did was remove myself from influencing their decisions. I wait to hear from them about what they fund." Her grandchildren range in age from 5 to 22. Their eligibility for the program ends at the age of 25, when she believes they should be capable of making donations on their own. When the youngest child in each fund reaches the age limit, the principal will revert to the community foundation "as a thank-you for dealing with these small funds."

bonds between them and teach children another perspective on giving. A good way to kick off the process is for the grandparents to share their views of philanthropy with their grandchildren and discuss how they have put their values into action in their own lives. In this way, the grandparents pass on the family legacy.

 TIP: To find the community foundation nearest you, visit **www.communityfoundationlocator.com** or consult the Council on Foundations Web site, **www.cof.org**, or phone 202/466-6512.

Grantmaking Tied to Faith

One year, Beth and Josh Bruner of Rochester, New York, wanted to introduce their 11-year-old son, Zac, to giving. They decided to forgo the usual Hanukkah gifts and put $5,000 into a donor-advised Jewish community foundation fund in Zac's name. Later, much of Zac's bar mitzvah money went into the fund, and his parents added to it as well. "It's an easy, wonderful tool that could also be done for a child's sixteenth birthday or other special occasion," Beth says.

"Each Friday night, when we have a Shabbat family dinner, we put our change into the tzedakah box," Beth explains. Then about four times a year, the family adds up the change for charity—usually around $50—the parents double the amount and that, too, is added to Zac's foundation account. Now 14, Zac reads financial statements, calls the community foundation to ask questions and decides how he will designate the interest from his fund.

Another option for children is the Jewish Fund for Justice, a national organization that helps young people under 21 fund projects that benefit youth. For a minimum donation of $1,000 plus a one-time administrative fee of $100, kids can have a Youth Endowment Fund. Some children use money they receive for their bar or bat mitzvahs. Others have funds endowed by their parents or other relatives. Each year the child receives a short list of projects supporting youth organizing groups. These groups work on issues affecting youth living in poor neighborhoods. The child then designates one project to receive the interest earned on his or her fund.

A Retreat for Young Donors

Catherine Gund, 34, who grew up in a wealthy philanthropic family, taps her personal experiences to help teens and young adults become effective givers. She became the youngest member of the George Gund Foundation board when she was 32. In 1996 Gund also cofounded the Third Wave Foundation, which raises money for grants to serve young women between the ages of 15 and 30, especially in education, reproductive rights and feminist, social-justice organizing. The Third Wave board is a mix of racially and economically diverse women and men.

Under the Third Wave umbrella, Gund helps organize an annual Young Donor Retreat that attracts participants who are mostly in their 20s, though some are as young as 14. Gund says the retreat appeals to young people who have wealth and a social conscience, who know they can use their money for good purposes but aren't sure how to do that.

"Young people haven't been taught to take their giving seriously, like some of their parents and grandparents. It's looked at as something only done by stodgy older men with cigars and cummerbunds." Gund remarks. "Young people should put themselves in that picture, wearing whatever's comfortable. They need to be organized and find out about groups and give to them in strategic ways—not just give $50 here and there to everybody." She explains that at the conference, "participants learn about the political, personal, technical and philanthropic aspects of having wealth, whether earned or inherited."

Gund notes that many of the retreat attendees grew up in families who never discussed their wealth. They may have seen their parents' pictures in the paper because of their philanthropy or know that their family name is on a building, but money wasn't discussed at home. Often, young people with wealth don't talk about it outside the family because they don't want to seem different from their friends who aren't as financially well-off.

Although Gund's mother is philanthropic and modeled it for her children, "there wasn't active training in how she went about it." Today, they work closely on some projects, but Gund began her philanthropic work through her political activism. "I worked with organizations that needed money," she says. Gund first got involved in giving through participation in a foundation that integrated fundraising and activism.

---

activity

Setting Priorities among Possible Donation Recipients

Mary Walachy, executive director of the Irene E. and George A. Davis Foundation in Springfield, Massachusetts, uses this exercise when she talks with grade-school classes (fourth grade and up) about the challenge donors face when choosing among several worthy causes. She says the children are always able, with little prompting from her, to weigh who and how many people will be helped and how much impact that help will have. Try using this exercise to start a conversation with kids about how to reach consensus and get the most impact from their limited dollars.

Task: You are a trustee of the Munger Hill Foundation. The purpose of your foundation is to provide funds to organizations that are dedicated to improving the quality of life of children. At today's meeting, you are being asked to review the following requests for funding. You have $50,000 to award this time.

Proposals:

1. The local boys and girls club is requesting $25,000 to start an educational program for local children. Called "Power Hour," the program will offer children between the ages of 8 and 18 homework help, tutoring and enrichment activities. The program hopes to serve 100 children in the first year.

As the first third-generation member to serve on the family foundation board (family members must be 30 or older to serve), she wants to introduce her own children—twin babies and a three-year-old—to philanthropy at a much earlier age. "I love seeing my babies crawling around the office while we make grants there," Gund says. "At this point, my daughter associates board meetings with seeing her aunts and uncles, and then watching a video in the back room. But as she grows older, she'll see this as a family business."

2. A local group of parents is requesting $40,000 to provide scholarships to students graduating from local high schools who have been accepted into college but do not have the money needed to attend. The scholarships are expected to help approximately 15 students.

3. The local hospital has requested $75,000 to pay for the cost of lifesaving equipment that is needed in the hospital's neonatal intensive care unit. This unit provides immediate medical services to infants who are born prematurely or experience severe birth complications that require intensive, life-saving medical interventions. This equipment will serve hundreds of infants born at the hospital for many years to come.

4. The local YMCA has requested $50,000 to provide scholarships for children and teens to attend summer camp and to pay for the costs of Y memberships for other needy children. The $50,000 will pay for 60 children to attend Y programs. Without the opportunity to attend camp, many of these children will spend the entire summer on the streets or unsupervised in their homes because their parents must work and are unable to pay for childcare. The Y staff feels strongly that many of the children and teens may get into serious trouble over the summer if they are not given opportunities to attend structured, organized activities that are both recreational and educational.

Strategic vs. From-the-Heart Giving

When philanthropists talk about strategic giving, they mean putting their money where it will do the most good. It's easy to overemphasize the point when guiding children. Tracy Gary, who wrote a popular book on how to create a giving plan, thinks kids should have the latitude to give spontaneously. "There's strategic giving but there's also giving from the heart," she says.

Fred Smith says that when he and his daughters passed a beggar on a Manhattan street corner and they wanted to give him money, "my first thought was no. But then I said it was a good idea. I didn't care if he spent it on wine. I was just happy to see them express the desire to help someone." He thinks parents should let their kids make some mistakes in their giving. "We can work on strategic giving later, once they develop the spirit of giving."

As children get older, you can start introducing the idea of effective giving. By helping children research a cause to which they want to give, they can find out:

—How solid the organization is (i.e., how long it has existed, whether it has strong leaders)
  —How the organization's programs address community needs
  —Who it serves (how many people annually)
  —Whether it has wide community support (donations and/or volunteers)
  —What it plans for the future

 TIP: The Women's Fund of the Milwaukee Foundation has created The Little Women's Fund, a concept that has inspired imitation by others. To honor an individual child, donors create growth-oriented endowments that mature, as the children grow, into charitable funds. When the children reach adulthood, they can designate gifts to the programs of their choice using the funds. Girls with funds in their names receive *The Giving Book,* a three-volume set of activities, stories and service projects covering age groups 5-8, 9-12 and 13-17. The curriculum teaches girls not only about sharing time and money but also about financial literacy. (See the Resources section for ordering information.)

CHAPTER SIX

From Classroom to Boardroom:
Building Youth Leadership
in Philanthropy

Every individual matters. Every individual has a role to play. Every individual makes a difference.

—JANE GOODALL

As more nonprofit organizations and family foundations recognize the value of youth involvement on their boards, new opportunities are being created for young people who want to start their community education early. Nonprofits providing services to youth are realizing that they are more effective when they hear directly from young people about what services are needed and how they should be designed. No matter the topic, young board members bring fresh perspectives, energy, creativity and ideas. And they may be more open to change than other board members are.

Nonprofits also recognize that today's youth should be taught volunteering and giving now if they are expected to become philanthropists as adults. That's one reason some major funders encourage grantees, especially those providing youth services, to involve youth in advisory roles. Another reason to involve young people is the rapidly growing number of family foundations. Many understand the need to get young family members involved so they will carry on the foundation's work later. (For more on what these foundations are doing, see chapter 7.)

By serving on boards, children learn to cooperate with others, experience being on an equal footing with adults, and gain an understanding of their community's needs and how they can contribute. Kids who've done it say it's a great experience.

You're Never Too Young

Often the programs that involve youth on boards are aimed at students in high school, or occasionally middle school students. But even elementary school children can participate if the activities are geared to their age.

An excellent example is provided by the Penny Harvest run by Common Cents, a nonprofit organization in New York City. Children raise their grant money, one penny at a time. And the majority on the Penny Harvest's grantmaking boards are kids in elementary school, some as young as kindergarten age.

During a three-week period each year, children, their parents and neighbors collect pennies. In 1999, 550 participating New York City schools collected nearly $400,000 this way. Schools that collect at least $1,000 can establish a student roundtable to decide how that money will be donated. The money collected by schools that don't meet the threshold is pooled in a fund administered by a citywide roundtable of high school students. The schools that contributed can apply for grants from the fund.

"It's a community-building project, and teachers like it because no one is excluded and no one's contribution is too small," says Common Cents Director Teddy Gross, who founded the program in 1991. The organization's operating expenses are paid by foundation grants, so the children get to allocate all the money they collect.

Common Cents trains the teachers, who lead their children through a process of identifying the community they want to serve—their school, their block, the planet. They then choose areas of concern to which they would like to contribute and re-search service organizations in those areas. Kindergarten students who participate work through "family roundtables" that also involve their parents.

For many kids, the site visits are the best part. "We give them little clipboards and work with the parents and teachers to come up with questions," explains Gross. One recent grant purchased an ironing board for a women's shelter that provides residents with clothes for job interviews. "The kids noticed the women were ironing their clothes on cots," Gross recalls. The students not only funded the ironing board but bought it and delivered it to the shelter. Others decided to replace a Scrabble game at a nursing home when they saw residents had substituted cardboard letters for missing tiles.

The children, many of whom live in poor neighborhoods, take their work very seriously. "It's sobering to have $1,000 and the job of giving it away responsibly," Gross says. "Most poor children never get the chance to do that."

For information on how to bring the Penny Harvest to your community, see the Resources section.

Community Foundations Involve Youth

Some 250 community foundations in 30 states are incorporating young people into advisory and grantmaking roles. And the numbers are growing, according to a database compiled by the Council of Michigan Foundations (CMF).

The CMF's Youth Project is the largest and most successful program for involving young people in grantmaking. Created in the 1980s in collaboration with the W. K. Kellogg Foundation, the project has trained hundreds of youth in fundraising and grantmaking.

The Kellogg Foundation launched the program by establishing challenge grants that would help community foundations respond to emerging needs, according to Jim McHale, who worked with the CMF project before joining the Kellogg Foundation as assis-

tant vice president. If a community foundation could get someone to donate unrestricted funds or field-of-interest funds (money
designated to an area such as art or education but without specific grantees suggested), the Kellogg Foundation would match
the donation at 50 cents for every dollar. The catch was that the
match had to go for youth services, and the community foundation had to form a youth advisory council (YAC) with at least half
the members under the age of 21.

Michigan now has 86 YACs that annually involve 1,500 students, most in high school but a few in junior high. The councils
have three responsibilities: assess the needs of the community's
young people, raise a portion of the funds to be matched, and
advise the community foundation board about where the income
of the youth endowment should go.

The Kids Proved Capable

"There was a little resistance at first" from some community
foundations, McHale recalls. "They wondered if they could trust
young people to make these decisions." Gradually, however, the
YACs proved that, with training, they not only were capable of
effective grantmaking, but contributed a different—and needed—
perspective.

As the YACs assessed community needs, for example, the foundations discovered that "what young people found as needs and
what adults perceived were two different things," McHale says.
Adults might identify teen pregnancy or high school dropout rates
as problems to be tackled. "But the young people cut to the chase
and focused on root causes." They'd point to the lack of a loving,
caring adult in a child's life or the lack of after-school or summer
programs to keep teenagers busy and out of trouble.

The Kellogg Foundation required that the youth participate in
fundraising, McHale says, "because these kids will be the future
members of the United Way board or a college board or the community hospital, and a big part of that is raising money. We wanted
them to learn how." Some organized events, but "many others

were involved in direct solicitation of CEOs of local companies. They asked for sizable gifts and were successful at it." The kids also are ambassadors for their community foundations. One donor who heard the students speak about their foundation work went home and immediately wrote a check for $150,000 to add to the YAC funds, McHale recalled.

YAC members learn to review grant requests, conduct site visits, interview grantees and make recommendations. "Some have the income off a million-dollar endowment, so they have serious money," McHale notes. Some YACs developed a reputation with grant applicants for being a harder sell than the community foundation's board "because they asked tougher questions and wanted more data on outcomes," McHale says. Effective youth involvement efforts must recognize that kids get bored if all they do is sit in a room and hear reports, McHale says. "Get them out in the field, meet with organizations, interview people," he advises. Seeing things firsthand is what excites young people.

Involving a More Diverse Group of Young People

In forming their YACs, most community foundations played it safe initially, choosing members of the National Honor Society or other school leaders. "When they started feeling comfortable, some started picking kids that haven't been traditionally involved," McHale explains. "I worked with one council in rural Northern Michigan that involved a kid who was flunking out of school and in trouble with the law. Once he got involved in the YAC, he worked into a leadership position and finished school." McHale recalls asking the teenager what turned things around. "He said, 'Jim, this is the first time anybody has asked me to do anything that really matters.'"

McHale saw kids as young as 12 serve on YACs. Some YACs have even created mini grant programs so elementary school children can try grantmaking. "We've seen that young people really do care and will take responsibility," McHale says. What they need are opportunity, training, support and permission to make mistakes. Some community foundations have given YACs grantmaking responsibilities for youth funds beyond those that were in the original project.

The program's ultimate goal "is to train a new generation of philanthropists," states CMF President and Chief Executive Officer Robert Collier. "We know from ten years of doing it that it's a wonderful builder of leadership skills and self-esteem. They are taught to be problem solvers and wise stewards. It also introduces them to a career option they may never have been exposed to. Some go on to college and become leaders in the nonprofit sector."

"The youth are smarter than we give them credit for," Collier says. "Trust them," McHale adds. They can do the right thing instinctively. He recalled working with a newly forming YAC composed of five middle-class white teens. "I asked them how they would design the board," he says. They decided to reach out to kids who weren't just like they were—including kids who could become recipients of the service—because they recognized they wouldn't be as effective without views and experiences beyond their own.

Grantmaking in Schools

The Surdna Foundation pioneered mini-foundations in the classroom in the early 1990s. Called the Student Service and Philanthropy Project (SSPP), the program included a high school course in which a classroom of students learned about philanthropy and grantmaking and then disbursed $1,500 to $2,500 provided by Surdna. The students also performed community service.

According to Robert Sherman, a program officer for Surdna, the SSPP was implemented in approximately 20 high schools in New York and a few other places around the country. When the project concluded after about five years, the curriculum concepts that had been developed were integrated into the Council of Michigan Foundations' K–12 Education in Philanthropy Project. (See chapter 3 for more on the K–12 curriculum.)

---

story

Giving Youth a Voice

Before working with the CMF Youth Project, Jim McHale was a fundraiser for a hospital. He volunteered to organize a summer camp for kids who were oncology patients. The camp had an adult board, which at one point decided to cut some programs that later were found to be rated most highly on the kids' evaluation surveys.

At that point, McHale started including young cancer patients on all the camp governance committees, even the Medical Committee composed of doctors and nurses. The doctors, for example, might create a schedule that would have a camper getting chemotherapy in the evening, causing him to miss a dance. A camper suggested a schedule change that would allow attendance at the dance first and treatment later. "The adults started listening to the young people, who felt they had a voice," McHale says.

Involving youth in planning and implementation of youth services entails a major change in the way nonprofits work, contends CMF's Robert Collier. "If they're going to do anything with youth, they need to talk to them."

The El Pomar Model

Colorado high school students in the El Pomar Foundation's Youth in Community Service (EPYCS) program have awarded close to $4 million to nonprofit organizations across their state since 1991. In the 1999–2000 school year alone, students in more than 100 high schools granted more than $825,000. Approximately half of all Colorado high school students are reached by the program.

Each EPYCS group is student-directed and supervised by a faculty advisor. El Pomar Foundation staff provide the know-how. If students raise $500, the foundation awards it a grant of $7,500.

Having the students put up some of the money helps develop their buy-in of the program. Some schools raise more than $500, adding to the funds they can use for grants. In addition to granting money to community nonprofits, they can give up to $2,500 to support clubs, programs or projects in their school.

Membership in EPYCS is open to all students in a participating school. Often it starts with student government leaders or a community service club, and they recruit others. As part of their work in EPYCS, students begin the school year by participating in a variety of community service projects. Afterward, the students convene to talk about their experiences. Another of the group's first tasks each fall is to survey the student body to identify the issues they feel are the most critical to their community and their school. From that survey, the students create a mission statement to help them establish a focus for their grantmaking.

The El Pomar staff conducts workshops to teach students about the nonprofit sector and how to make grants. They learn how to evaluate a proposal, interview the staff of potential grantees and decide among competing grant requests. "Most of the students have never had the opportunity to give money away, so you can't assume they have knowledge about philanthropy or making grants," says Gary Butterworth, program director. "One of the lessons they learn is how to stretch their dollars to have the most impact," Butterworth notes. "It's a problem-solving exercise. The kids get 100 or more proposals; $8,000 seems like a lot at first, but with so many great organizations, it's hard to pare them down."

Not every grant works out as the students hope, and there's a lesson in that too. Occasionally projects have failed, or funded nonprofits have folded. "When that happens, students have the opportunity to learn from past mistakes," Butterworth explains. "Many times the result is students' conducting site visits to organizations to ensure effective grantmaking."

For Jayme Holligan, a graduate of Palmer High School in Colorado Springs, one highlight of her three years in EPYCS was the year-end ceremony at which representatives from each high school

---

story

One Student's Experience

Heather Sharkey, who graduated from Palmer High School in Colorado Springs in 2000, chaired her school's EPYCS board in her senior year. "Not only did it make me more aware of the needs in the community but it also gave me more confidence to go out and mix it up with adults and find out where I can be of service," Sharkey says. She also found evaluating grantees to be an empowering experience. When applicants send a representative to sell the students on their organization, "you feel you have a good deal of power and responsibility. It's a flip from our usual experience, where we're going to organizations and asking for donations for the football team or whatever. We also learned how to budget money, work with community leaders and say 'no' in a polite and caring way."

Sharkey's group combined site visits with volunteering. "We served food at the Red Cross shelter, worked on housing projects and visited nursing homes," she explains. "Instead of just going to the soup kitchen and looking at what they do, it's easier if you are in there working." Some students continued volunteering at sites they visited, especially at the Red Cross. "Some of the children who live at the Red Cross shelter go to our high school," Sharkey adds.

She believes that students too often "don't feel valued by adults or important or needed in their community. Students aren't always respectful, which perpetuates the cycle. EPYCS is an opportunity for students to affirm what kids can do."

---

present checks to representatives of the nonprofits they've decided to fund. The biggest challenge, she says, was "collaborating with my peers" to make the tough choices of which groups to fund. "It took teamwork, listening and focusing on our goals." She has continued her community service efforts at the University of Colorado. "I probably wouldn't have had the same interest without El Pomar," she says. "I would not be the same person."

TIP: If you'd like students in your child's school to be able to make grants, El Pomar will share its curriculum with you (see the Resources section). Consider approaching foundations in your community about funding replication of the El Pomar model. For the names of local foundations, consult the Foundation Center's directory. Many public libraries have copies, or you can visit the Web site **www.Foundation Center.org**.

Training Young Trustees

Many youth groups, after-school programs and even community foundations want to create student boards but need training, for both their leaders and the students. Community Partnerships with Youth, Inc. (CPY), in Fort Wayne, Indiana, is a leader in fulfilling those training needs. CPY teaches trusteeship, governance and philanthropy primarily to youth aged 11 to 18. The materials on philanthropy are available to use with children as young as 5 years old.

"We go beyond leadership training," says Anne Hoover, CPY's executive director. "We're not just building skills but working on the inner you," by helping children form their belief system. One of their first steps is helping young people write a personal mission statement. Hoover defines trusteeship as leadership with a heart. "It's serving the common good of the community." Those young people who move beyond community service and take a governance role on a board need to acquire additional skills so they understand financial statements, agendas, conflict resolution and consensus building.

Hoover says some adults like the idea of having youth on boards in theory but have trouble dealing with it in practice. "What we like best is training both youth and adults." She stresses that boards must be prepared to give young people meaningful work to do immediately following the training. "With young people, training is only the beginning. Kids like to put their training into action as soon as possible," Hoover explains.

CPY's curriculum materials and training workshops for youth professionals were written by educators and funded by the Lilly

Endowment, which supports youth involvement across Indiana. (See the Resources section for information on CPY's offerings.)

Dealing with Intergenerational Issues

When youth members are added to an adult board, the young people may feel intimidated, be reluctant to ask questions and not understand the board's jargon. If they feel they are being treated as kids instead of full-fledged board members, they may want to quit. Adding young people to a board requires a culture change.

Youth on Board, a Boston-based organization started in 1994 with a W. K. Kellogg Foundation grant, helps ease the transition. They train youth in board governance and work with the adults to determine how the board's policies and practices—such as meeting schedules—could be changed to make youth service easier.

Sometimes Youth on Board suggests that an adult member be assigned to mentor a young member. But, advises cofounder Karen Young, "mentoring should be a back-and-forth relationship. Adults need to know about young people's lives and what the world is like to them. Young members want guides, not bosses."

Tips from Youth on Board for adult boards that want to include youth:

—Understand your motivation. Do you want to be true partners with young people in decisionmaking?

—Be prepared to commit the board and staff time needed to make the process work well.

—Make sure your meeting structure encourages all members to express their views.

—Have ongoing training about intergenerational relationships.

(See the Resources section for more information about Youth on Board.)

Seventh Graders Leverage $2,500 into Half a Million Dollars

Michael Kesselman thought bar and bat mitzvah celebrations were getting out of hand. Social pressure to host lavish parties had grown up around this important Jewish ceremony marking a young person's coming of age. As the second of his three daughters neared her thirteenth birthday, he decided to propose a radical change.

"My wife and I calculated that we'd have to spend $18 to $20 times 33 [the number of students in his daughter's Jewish day-school class] on gifts that year," Kesselman recalls. Since each student invited the entire class to each celebration, Kesselman calculated that, collectively, the seventh grade parents would spend about $20,000 on gifts. "My eldest daughter, Talya, had her bat mitzvah five years earlier," Kesselman says. "I asked her, 'What do you remember about your gifts?'" Talya could recall only one or two things she received.

So Kesselman, deputy director for programs at the Koret Foundation in San Francisco, wrote a letter to the other parents in daughter Iva's class proposing two alternatives to multiple gift buying. "First, I put together a cost estimate for a weekend party at an amusement park including food, lodging, passes to get in . . . everything," he explains. In addition to the party, he proposed a second alternative much more to his liking: "I said, 'Let's put money into a fund. The kids will be the board,'" and he would volunteer to help them run it like a foundation.

The families chose the latter proposal. Each family that was financially able was asked to put in $300. Half of that went to the corpus of the Seventh Grade Fund (for a total of $4,500). The other $150 per family went into an account that would provide each student a $100 check from the whole class for the bar or bat mitzvah plus a more personal gift—a handcrafted tzedakah box with the recipient's name engraved on it in Hebrew. "The box was connected to what the ceremony means: that you are now responsible for the community, not just yourself, because now you are an adult," Kesselman explains. If a student wasn't going to have a bar mitzvah, the check and box would be presented for his birthday.

Next came the job of helping the students give away their $4,500 fund. "I told the kids, 'I work for you,'" Kesselman remembers. "I gave them all the information, but I let them make all the decisions." During lunch hours, the board—which included the whole class—met to choose the areas on which they would focus their grants.

One of their first interests was an interfaith project to save housing on a military facility that was about to be torn down. Religious groups wanted to save it for the homeless. Kesselman got a prominent rabbi and a leader of the local Muslim community to make a presentation to the students about the project.

Meanwhile, several organizations in the San Francisco Bay area contributed to the fund after Kesselman explained that the students had given up gifts to support good works. Kesselman felt that, with more publicity, additional funders would help out. He sent press releases to 30 news outlets and got only one response—from the *San Francisco Chronicle*, which played the story, with photographs, on the front page under the headline "Taking the Torah to Heart." ABC News then gave the story national coverage, and encouraging letters with checks from individual donors started arriving.

Soon the fund grew to $13,000 and the seventh graders were busy weighing funding requests and going on site visits. To teach them strategic philanthropy, Kesselman explained how to leverage funds. A 20-year-old who wanted to bike from San Francisco to Los Angeles for AIDS research asked the kids to sponsor him. "He explained that he had been successfully treated for a brain tumor and had vowed to help sick people when he recovered," Kesselman recounts. "I suggested

(continues)

continued

they make it a challenge grant. I said 'You could give him $500 if he raises $1,000.'" The bicyclist exceeded the challenge.

Similarly, the kids wanted to make a grant of $1,500 for Kosovo refugee relief through American Jewish World Service (AJWS). Kesselman suggested that AJWS use the Seventh Grade Fund's grant as a challenge to other middle schools. AJWS raised more than twice as much as the grant and told many other children about the refugees' plight than they might have otherwise.

The biggest payoff came because the kids were interested in reducing domestic violence. "I was very surprised," Kesselman says. "These were middle and upper class kids, and they wanted to focus on child abuse." The director of La Casa de las Madres, a shelter for battered women, had made a presentation asking for $2,500. Aided by Kesselman's knowledge of the foundation world, the class and the shelter director started dreaming bigger. Kesselman told them about the Robert Wood Johnson Foundation's Local Initiative Funding Partners Program, which matches funds raised by consortia of local foundations.

The Seventh Grade Fund learned that there was little help for teens living in domestic violence situations. La Casa put together a proposal for the Robert Wood Johnson Foundation to match $240,000 raised locally over three years. The Seventh Grade Fund would be the lead local funding agent, and La Casa would use the money to provide teen services. Within two weeks, Kesselman lined up 12 local foundations for a meeting to discuss the proposal. When the Robert Wood Johnson Foundation conducted a site visit and met the funders, five 13-year-olds represented the Seventh Grade Fund. The mayor sent a representative to say that the city would try to keep the program going after the three-year start-up phase.

Competition for the Robert Wood Johnson Foundation grant money was stiff; hundreds of project recommendations were submitted from across the country. But the foundation's representatives were impressed with the students' proposal and awarded their partnership $225,000 in matching funds.

When the year was over, the students had learned important lessons about making grants. Aaron Keyak, one of the board members, found having to reject people was the hardest part. "I ended up voting against the request from a rabbi I liked who's a friend of my family," Keyak says. One of the best parts was "learning how a board works. Now I'm on other boards." He has high praise for Kesselman, who helped the students but let them take the lead. When adults made presentations seeking the students' assistance, "it was mind-boggling for the kids," Kesselman says. "These people were talking to them because they could do something about a problem. It was empowering."

The students also learned to work together to make decisions. There often were winners and losers among the board members when the final vote was taken, sometimes creating bad feelings, but they learned to work it out. "We all had our own views," says Kesselman's daughter Iva. "But, in the end, we agreed on some important things."

Although some students weren't sold on the idea in the beginning, the class eventually shared a real sense of pride in the work they were doing, she says. "Kids are not born being philanthropic," her father adds. "This kind of project teaches them values that are very important. They learned philanthropy is more than just giving money away."

CHAPTER SEVEN

Passing the Torch: Using Ideas from Family Foundations

The untapped potential of America's families to further address community needs is astounding.

—WILLIAM RICHARDSON, CHAIRMAN AND CEO
W. K. KELLOGG FOUNDATION

It's predicted that as baby boomers inherit their parents' estates, upwards of $12 trillion in wealth will be transferred intergenerationally in the next 20 years. The rapidly growing number of family foundations, which are private foundations governed by a family, is one result of this shift in wealth and the desire to see it put to effective use for the good of society. There are approximately 30,000 family foundations in the United States giving an estimated $7 billion a year.

There are easier, less time-consuming ways for families to donate money than through family foundations, which require a greater financial and administrative commitment than other philanthropic options. Yet many are drawn to this vehicle for giving precisely because it provides an ongoing commitment for family members. The foundation provides a bond that connects families across generations and through the years.

Often, family members from two or three generations serve together as trustees to make decisions about grants. As families become dispersed geographically, foundation meetings provide regular opportunities for members to meet, for cousins to get to know each other better, for grandparents to stay in touch with their grandchildren. Families can, of course, get together without creating a foundation. But doing so also provides a structure in which an extended family can collaborate, even when they don't live near each other. Members can strengthen their relationships as they discuss their family's values, the needs of their community and their priorities when choosing grantees.

Another potential benefit of having a family foundation is that it can provide opportunities for youth to learn about philanthropy. Although in some states trustees must be either 18 or 21 (check your state's laws regarding age of trustees), some foundations are involving children earlier in various ways, either informally or as student advisers or junior board members. By the time they work together as adults on the family foundation board, the younger generation has already had a chance to develop trusting relationships with each other and with their older relatives.

It's not always easy to know exactly how to fit children in the picture, as we saw in the previous chapter. But many family foundations are trying innovative ways to do so. By engaging children early in their lives, gradually increasing the connection as they move through their teenage years, the odds are better that this generation will remain active in the foundation in adulthood.

This doesn't mean children have to sit at the table and help make funding decisions—although that's one option. Children can be exposed to the foundation in a variety of ways. Granted, it takes effort on the part of foundation staff (if there are any) or family members to create opportunities to connect with children. But families who make the effort say it pays off later when young, energetic members make a smooth transition to the adult board because they've already learned the ropes in childhood.

Even if you don't have a family foundation, you can adapt some of the creative ideas described in this chapter to use in your own family giving efforts.

TIP: For information on starting a family foundation, contact the
Council on Foundations at **www.cof.org** or 202/466-6512.

Attending Meetings

Few children want to sit in a stuffy board room while adults
discuss their foundation's financial and administrative matters.
But, depending on the children's ages and level of interest, visiting a board meeting occasionally—and having the option to stay
only for a portion of the discussion—may get a surprising number of takers. Kids like to see the world adults operate in, especially their parents. Just as it's fun to drop in on Mom's or Dad's
workplace, looking in on meetings to watch parents, grandparents, aunts or uncles work together on a project appeals to some
children.

RuthAnne Anderson started attending meetings of her family's
Harris Foundation in Houston when she was five. She remembers trying hard to sit still and "being bored stiff. But the thing
that got my attention was when my Aunt Marilyn would do the
postgrant reports. It was like listening to stories with many happy
endings." The postgrant reports and the thank-you notes read by
her brother remain the highlight of board meetings for her in
adulthood.

Some foundations combine annual meetings with family reunions. These can create opportunities to engage even the very
young. Alternating recreation activities with several short, seg-
mented business sessions recognizes children's limited attention
span. Some foundations schedule these meetings at Thanksgiving, so families can tie their philanthropy with being thankful for
their many blessings—a concept children can readily grasp.

Every two years, The Frees Foundation of Houston meets some-
place where all family members can have fun when they aren't
conducting board and foundation business. The five-day meetings allow time for horseback riding, swimming, site visits and
grantmaking. On alternate years, the foundation's annual meeting is held by telephone conference call. The first part of the

meeting is devoted to reports on grants made by the younger members of the foundation. That way, the kids who don't want to sit through the whole meeting can leave the call after the part they are most interested in.

In the Foss Foundation of Sonoma, California, any descendant of the founders can be a member of the foundation and participate in the annual meeting as long as that person signs up every year. The only limitation is that those under 18 are associate members and can't vote in the election of board members. Even those who are too young to grasp what's going on can feel part of the family endeavor. "We hire babysitters for the younger ones, but they are in the room for some of the meeting, usually on the floor doing art work," says Virginia Hubbell, who staffs the foundation.

 TIP: Foundations that combine their board meetings with family vacations or reunions need to be especially careful to avoid violating the legal prohibition on expenditures that benefit family members. A foundation may reimburse *reasonable* and *necessary* expenses that family members incur in providing services to the foundation, including the expense of attending board meetings. However, while holding a board meeting is necessary, the IRS may question whether it was reasonable to hold that meeting at an exotic vacation destination. Moreover, only the family members who sit on the board are entitled to reimbursement. A foundation cannot reimburse travel expenses for a family member's spouse or children unless the person being reimbursed is performing necessary services for the foundation. Families that want to combine board meetings with vacations should consider footing their own expenses, or they should consult with experienced outside counsel to determine whether expenditures that the foundation will reimburse meet the reasonable-and-necessary test.

Sarah Stranahan, chair of the Needmor Foundation based in Boulder, Colorado, has taken her 11- and 12-year-old sons on site visits. She takes one along when she travels from her New York City home to the foundation meetings. "I want them to know what Mom does that makes her so busy all the time," she explains. They're also gaining familiarity with the language and the process at board meetings. They don't have to participate. Sometimes they'll listen for a while and then go back to the hotel and read."

Stranahan enjoyed attending foundation gatherings when she was young. The attraction was hanging out with her cousins. "We'd stay up, and talk. We had a lot in common: the same grandparents, inherited money, the same culture." Stranahan doesn't think a family should "force the foundation down the throats" of members' children, however. The family had discussed having a "Needmor Camp," in which all the children would learn the basics about the foundation. "We decided Needmor Camp was the worst thing we could do," she says. Instead, her generation strives to create a welcoming atmosphere that allows each child to set a pace in being exposed to the family's philanthropy.

 TIP: Here's something to try the next time your family gathering includes young children. Jim Harrell, a vice president at Northern Trust Bank in Dallas, presents a philanthropy workshop for the younger set each year at the Conference of Southwest Foundations' annual meeting. Using his skills as a former first-grade teacher, he asks the kids to identify community helpers. The children will list police officers, librarians, nurses, firefighters, teachers. Then he leads a discussion about what these helpers do and where they work—such as hospitals, schools, libraries—places that could be grant recipients. He has the children pick their favorite helpers, draw pictures of them, cut them out and glue them onto a large sheet of butcher paper. The children then draw the workplaces. Finally, they discuss how they chose their favorite helpers in an exercise that resembles the grantmaking that their families' foundations do. "They can understand," Harrell says. "You just have to meet them on their level."

Junior Boards

Some family foundations have junior boards comprising young adults. Others are dipping into the ranks of their youngest family members, either adding them to the junior board or setting up a separate panel just for them.

---

story

The Cousin Fund

California's June & Julian Foss Foundation gives the phrase "You're never too young" new meaning. The board of its Cousin Fund has no minimum-age requirement, only the stipulation that a child be old enough to read and make a conscious choice to participate. The current group brings together 21 members of the third generation, who range in age from 10 to the late 30s.

The cousins have $20,000 to allocate annually. Their choices then go to the Foss Foundation board (their parents and grandparents) for final approval. Sometimes the board augments the grants, which must fall within the foundation's broad mission—serving children and youth.

The two cochairs of the fund are the youngest and the oldest cousins. About 50 percent of the Cousin Fund members are still in school or college, according to the foundation's administrator, Virginia Hubbell. She screens proposals for the group based on the interests the cousins have expressed. The Cousin Fund uses e-mail to discuss proposals, because face-to-face meetings with young people who live all over the country are difficult to arrange. But every proposal being considered gets a site visit from a cousin and Hubbell before the group makes its final decisions. The cousin who makes the visit writes a report for the others to review and gets to make the call informing an organization that it's funded.

Usually a junior board is given a fund to allocate to grantees in much the same way that the senior board does. Although the trustees on the senior board must sign off on the junior board's allocations because foundation funds are being expended, the best arrangements honor the junior board's choices so the youth feel their views are accepted. Some are told they must choose grantees that fall within the foundation's mission, but others are allowed to fund any charitable group.

The Frees Foundation Model

Nancy Frees was disheartened to learn that by the fourth generation, many foundation boards have a minority of members from the family, because later generations lose interest. Her parents, who had endowed The Frees Foundation, were still living, and Nancy wanted to make sure their legacy would continue in the hands of their descendents.

She was the driving force behind the creation in the early 1990s of the Houston foundation's junior advisory board for young people aged 10 to 21. "We try to make their training experience as real as possible," Frees says. Not only do the youth board members decide on grant allocations, they also have their own investment portfolio. They learn about investments and follow their portfolio's performance in the same way the senior board members do. "We wanted them to learn about financial responsibility as well as philanthropy," Frees explained. In addition, junior board members are required to perform volunteer work "so they learn that philanthropy is not just money but perspiration," Frees says.

Each child has an allocation from which to make grants in his or her local community as well as nationally and internationally. This wide perspective challenges the members to search more broadly for grantees. They've even made international site visits, including one to Guatemala to see Frees Foundation projects supporting education for girls and village banking for women.

The junior board started with three members. The youngest was 11 and the oldest was ready to enter college. Now the oldest

---

story

Kids Clubs

A simplified version of a junior board is a Kids Club. Lynette Malinger, executive director of the Albert J. Speh, Jr., and Claire R. Speh Foundation, which was started by her grandfather, created one in 1998 for her nieces and nephews between the ages of 8 and 18.

Although the kids have $5,000 for grantmaking, their focus is on volunteering. Malinger helps them find volunteer opportunities that the children can do with their parents in the Chicago area, where most of the family lives. Activities are scheduled during the summer so the two Kids Club members in Florida can travel to participate. The Kids Club has helped clean an inner city school, worked at a soup kitchen and assisted with a carnival benefiting children affected by HIV/AIDS. The volunteer work has been so much fun that the members' friends have asked to participate too.

---

is out of college and is the first member of the third generation to serve on the senior board. She's also the liaison to the junior board, scheduling their conference calls and helping the members meet their grantmaking deadlines. When she is joined on the senior board by her sibling and cousins, each of them will bring 11 years of training to the table.

Adults Learn from the Kids

A junior board can enrich senior board members' service. For adults, the best part of the Harris Foundation's June retreat is the meeting of its student advisors, family members between the ages of 8 and 18. Each advisor is allowed to allocate about $1,500 a year to any organization. During the meeting, "each child shares who they gave to, why and what they hope to accomplish," explains RuthAnne Anderson, one of the foundation's trustees and mother of two student advisors, eight- and ten-year-old boys. Even though the meeting is for the children, the adult relatives attend because "we love to hear what they gave to and what they learned," Anderson says. "We also love to hear the family history," which her mom or another trustee reviews with the children each year.

Anderson helps her children make grant decisions in their community of Rome, Georgia, by taking them on field trips where she, too, learns about local needs and resources. When the family toured the Boys and Girls Club, Anderson's older son, Cody, observed that the kids in the after-school program needed a new foosball table to replace one that was falling apart. Her younger son found out the YMCA where he played baseball needed an ice machine for its concession stand. His mom helped him find a used one he could afford to purchase with his grant money.

Nancy Frees insists that the kids involved in her family's foundation "help us keep an open mind and a fresh perspective." Their presence also helps keep the foundation board meetings on an even keel, because the adults know they must be seen as role models for the kids. In some foundations, where the first and second generations can have serious disagreement, "bringing in the third generation keeps the discussion on a higher road."

Site Visits

Long before children make their own grants, they can go on site visits with their parents or with the staff (if there is one) of their family's foundation.

Lynette Malinger of the Speh Foundation helps members of the foundation's Kids Club hone their observational skills when on a site visit. She encourages the children to notice whether the facility is clean and has accommodations for disabled people, whether there are people of different races and ethnicity and

Site Visit Checklist

Lynette Malinger of the Speh Foundation put together this checklist for the children in her foundation's Kids Club to use on site visits.

Organization: _____

Amount Requested: _____

Purpose of Request: _____

Questions to ask yourself and discuss with other Kids Club kids:
1. Do you think that the people you talked with had good leadership skills to make the program or organization a success?
2. Is the place clean and safe for children? Did the children you saw look happy and busy?
3. Will our involvement (money or time) help the organization succeed in getting more people, other than us, to help?
4. Is there a better way to help, besides what they are asking for?
5. Does this help our goal of helping kids do their best?

Questions to ask the people at the agency:
1. How many kids come here this year? How many do you want to come next year?
2. How do the kids get to the agency? How do they hear about you?
3. What are some things that might be bothering the kids that come to the agency? What are they worried about?
4. What does it cost to come here, and how do the kids pay for it?
5. What do you like best about your agency, and what do you think makes it help kids?

When we get back to the office, you can fill out the form and discuss it with each other.

Strengths (What did you like best? What seemed to work well?):

_____

Weaknesses (Did you see anything that was a problem, or that you didn't think was good?): _____

whether they are mixing well. "They were shy at first about asking questions," she recalls, but they become more comfortable with experience. Sometimes, the Kids Club members play with the children at the facilities they visit. Malinger occasionally worries about safety. "If I'm nervous about going to a place I'm reviewing, I don't take them."

Helen Hunt, who created the New York-based Sister Fund to help women around the country, started taking her six children on site visits and to neighborhood meetings when they were babies. "I made the decision not to force philanthropy on my kids but to gently expose them to it," she explains. "If they were inclined in that direction, fine." Hunt wanted her children to see people "in a context different from their own." Site visits gave her the vehicle. Her children saw what it was like to be poor or homeless and they met people "who had the courage to overcome their barriers."

Keeping Kids Informed

If there's one thing kids love, it's getting mail (or e-mail). Just as foundations often produce newsletters for far-flung family members, some produce mailings specifically for the children in the family.

Trustee advisor RuthAnne Anderson edits a newsletter for the Harris Foundation's student advisors. The kids named it Toucan You Can! in honor of their favorite bird. (The foundation is a donor to the San Diego Zoo, wildlife preservation organizations and animal rescue groups.) She includes news about what the kids in the family are doing, what projects they are funding and what the foundation is up to. Using a scanner, she's able to incorporate photos and children's art work. She even includes word-search puzzles and poetry.

The children also receive occasional mailings from the foundation's staff member on grantees or other subjects she thinks they'd be interested in. She mails separate copies to children in the same family so all can open their own correspondence.

Passing the Torch

Families that want later generations to preserve the foundation should expose their children early to the family's and foundation's history and the intent of the donors. Some families use their annual gatherings to tell stories of the donors or, if they are alive, the donors themselves tell the younger generation what philanthropy means to them and how they've acted on that commitment.

Thirteen-year-old Jillian Foss is cochair of the Foss Family Foundation's Cousin Fund. When Jillian was 11, she teamed with her then 13-year-old cousin Jamie to write and illustrate a book about philanthropy to present at the annual meeting. "It tells what a foundation is, what philanthropy is, and talks about how Grampa planted the seed and a tree grew and now they have apples to share," says Virginia Hubbell.

Another activity at Foss family meetings is creating a large-scale artwork. Every family member is asked to record some thoughts on a piece of canvas. "The littlest ones scribble and others write a statement about their participation in the foundation," Hubbell explains. The canvas becomes a permanent record of the family.

When Bill Graustein, trustee of the William Caspar Graustein Foundation, was growing up, he often heard stories about his father's family told as fables with a moral. Years later, when he passed on the family stories to his two daughters, he saw the tales in a new light. To preserve them, he has recorded one of the stories for his daughters and written about others in the foundation's annual report. The Pueblo Indian figure of a storyteller is the logo of the foundation. Graustein says, "Our stories are part of the way we map our cultural understanding and make sense of our experience so we can navigate through the world."

Some foundations produce videotapes so the donors' legacy and stories will live on after they are gone. These may be elaborately produced by specialized companies or be as simple as home videos made during family gatherings. Making a video of their grandparents is a project the children in the family can undertake. Children can also help adult relatives compile family trees, histories and photo albums.

Internships

Children, especially teenagers, find internships a valuable way to take a crash course in foundation management. If they are allowed to shadow the staff for a month in the summer, or even a week, they'll learn what kinds of questions to ask on a site visit, what a grant proposal looks like and how to evaluate and prioritize funding requests.

Sally Klingenstein, executive director of the Klingenstein Third Generation Foundation, invited her 12-year-old niece to spend a week with her in the summer of 1999. "She's mature and was very interested," Klingenstein says. Her niece learned what it means to run a foundation. She read proposals, met potential grantees and evaluated a Web site for kids that the foundation had funded.

One of the groups the niece visited was Art Start, through which volunteers teach art in homeless shelters. She met one of the artists and told her aunt later, "That's amazing; this person isn't getting paid and he's put so much time into it," Klingenstein recalls. "She totally got that. I didn't have to say this is why we fund nonprofits."

Klingenstein doesn't believe all 12-year-olds are ready for such an experience. "Her father initiated the idea because he thought she was ready," Klingenstein explains. To help his daughter be taken seriously, he bought her a suit and had notepads printed with her name and title: "foundation assistant."

More common are high-school-age interns. Bruce Maza, executive director of the C. E. and S. Foundation in Louisville, Kentucky, hosted a high school senior from New Jersey during spring break in 2000. The internship focused on the intersection of public policy, public service and organized philanthropy, and introduced the intern to the day-to-day workings of a family foundation. "The foundation is deeply committed to internships with young people," Maza adds. "We want to do this much more. The perspective that young minds bring to our work is often enlightening."

One of the projects the C. E. and S. Foundation funds is Bulldogs in the Bluegrass, which brings 40 undergraduates from Yale to summer internships throughout the spectrum of Louisville's nonprofit community. "We find that these talented young people are often surprised and inspired and challenged to discover the breadth of enterprise and creativity exhibited by the array of nonprofit organizations, professionals and volunteers they meet here," Maza says. "The students tell us that their Louisville summer changes their lives."

Next Steps

By now you may be feeling stimulated and challenged by all the ideas and suggestions we've offered for involving your children in philanthropy. Perhaps the best advice we can give is to try it a little at a time. If you want to volunteer as a family, for example, you might set a goal of doing this quarterly, if that fits your family's schedule better than a monthly commitment. Recognize, too, that this is a process that can evolve over time as your child passes through various developmental stages and levels of interest.

In the foreword to this book, we listed some key steps to being a philanthropic mentor for your children. They are worth repeating here:

1. Be a role model—a volunteer and a donor.
2. Show kids the way—take them with you to volunteer; talk to them about your donations.
3. Make giving a year-round project, not just something to do at holidays.
4. Start now. The earlier you teach the habit of giving, the easier it will be to sustain.
5. Expect your children to serve and give.
6. Let children decide what projects to support with their money and time.
7. Teach them to manage money.
8. Praise them for their philanthropic actions.

If you keep these in mind, your children's philanthropic education will come naturally. And the benefits will extend far beyond
your own family. Philanthropy and service are key tools in fur-
thering democracy. If we raise kids who care about others, we'll
have passed on a legacy that will strengthen our communities
and make all families healthier and happier.

Resources
(arranged by topic)

Board Service:

Community Partnerships with Youth, Inc. A national training and resource development organization dedicated to promoting active citizenship through youth and adult partnerships. Offers curricula and workshops for youth and professionals. The training enables young people to become trustees of their communities and to serve on boards. 6319 Constitution Drive, Fort Wayne, IN 46804; 219/436-4402; **www.cpyinc.org**.

Points of Light Foundation. Develops models of youth involvement on boards and councils. Provides training to young people and organizations. 1400 Eye St., NW, Suite 800, Washington, DC 20005; 202/729-8000; **www.pointsoflight.org**.

Youth on Board. Provides training, consultation and materials on how to build effective intergenerational boards. P.O. Box 440322, Somerville, MA 02144; 617/623-9900; **www.youthonboard.org**.

Children's Books with Philanthropy Themes:

(To read to children in the age range of four to eight, although some children younger or older enjoy them too!)

Abiyoyo by Pete Seeger (Macmillan, 1986). African father and his son use the magic of song to save their village from a giant.

Kids' Random Acts of Kindness edited by Dawna Markova (Canari Press, 1994). Heartwarming stories of good deeds.

The Legend of Blue Bonnet by Tomie de Paola (G. P. Putnam's Sons, 1981). An orphaned Native American child gives her only possession to end a famine.

"The Lion and the Mouse." There are several versions of this Aesop fable, in which a lion spares a mouse from harm and the mouse has the opportunity to reciprocate.

Miss Rumphius by Barbara Cooney (Scholastic, 1985). Miss Rumphius teaches her niece to make the world more beautiful as she scatters lupine seeds everywhere she goes, leaving a legacy of blue flowers.

The Rainbow Fish by Marcus Pfister (North-South Books, 1992). A beautiful fish gives away its scales so other fish can be beautiful too.

"Stone Soup." There are several illustrated versions that retell this old story of a soup that started out with only a stone and water but ended up full of flavorful ingredients, thanks to the contributions of others.

Swimmy by Leo Lionni (Scholastic, 1963). Fish learn they can accomplish more if they act together.

Thidwick: The Big-Hearted Moose by Dr. Seuss (Random House, 1948). One of several Dr. Seuss books with themes of caring and helping others. Thidwick shelters and cares for other animals in his antlers.

Grantmaking:

Common Cents New York. Partners with schools to create real-world philanthropic opportunities. Children collect millions of pennies annually and use them to make grants (Penny Harvest). The organization is now extending its projects in communities beyond its original New York City base. 104 West 88th St., New York, NY 10024; 212/579-0579; **www.commoncents.org**.

Inspired Philanthropy by Tracy Gary and Melissa Kohner (Chardon Press, 1998). A workbook that helps adults explore their personal philanthropic values and create a giving plan. The book is helpful to parents who want to impart their values to their children by helping them crystallize their ideas on those values.

Look What Kids Can Do: Youth in Philanthropy (The Conference of Southwest Foundations, 1997). This book has detailed listings of organizations and projects providing opportunities for youth to engage in philanthropy. Includes youth on boards, as grantmakers and as volunteers. To purchase, contact CSF, 3102 Maple Ave., Suite 260, Dallas, TX 75201; 214/740-1787.

Michigan Community Foundations' Youth Project. A leading program to involve young people in grantmaking through community foundations. Numerous materials are available for downloading on its Web site, **www.mcfyp.org**, for communities that want to replicate this model. Council of Michigan Foundations, 1 South Harbor Ave., Suite 3, Grand Haven, MI 49417; 616/842-7080.

El Pomar Youth in Community Service Program. A project of the El Pomar Foundation, EPYCS works with schools in Colorado to create student boards and, through them, to make grants to community organizations. Makes its curriculum available for replication projects. 10 Lake Circle, Colorado Springs, CO 80906; 800/554-7711; **www.elpomar.org**.

Resource Generation. An alliance of young people (ages 21–32) who are donors and activists for social and economic justice. The alliance offers a guide, *Money Talks. So Can We*, about the personal, political and philanthropic aspects of wealth. Both the guide and the Web site list many other resources. P.O. Box 400336, North Cambridge, MA 02140; 617/441-5567; **www.resourcegeneration.org**.

Youth as Resources. Provides small grants to young people affiliated with youth centers, schools, churches and community foundations as they create projects to address social problems. 1700 K St., NW, Washington, DC 20006; 202/261-4185; **www.yar.org**.

Money Management:

Dollars and Sense for Kids (Kiplinger, 1999). Advice from Janet Bodnar for parents of preschool- through college-age kids. Helps you communicate with your children so they grow up with a healthy attitude toward money and have the ability to manage it. See also the Web site **www.kiplinger.com** for her column and other articles about kids and money.

The Jump$tart Coalition for Personal Financial Literacy. Jump$tart evaluates the financial literacy of young adults; develops, disseminates and encourages teaching of personal finance materials in grades K–12. 919 18th St., NW, Suite 300; Washington, DC 20006; 888/45-EDUCATE; **www.jumpstartcoalition.org**.

Money, Meaning and Choices Institute. A San Francisco-area consulting firm that advises individuals and families about the psychological challenges—and opportunities—of having or inheriting money. P.O. Box 803, Kentfield, CA 94914; 415/267-6107.

Money Management Seminars:

Girls, Inc. Runs a money management program for girls ages 6–18. The ten weekly sessions are taught at 1,000 sites nationwide.

120 Wall St., 3rd Floor, New York, NY 10005; 212/509-2000; **www.girlsinc.org**.

Independent Means. Offers ClubInvest, five-day seminars for 14- to 21-year-olds. Features on the Independent Means' Web site include an on-line forum on which girls can chat with financial role models and see news clips on saving and investing. 126 Powers Ave., Santa Barbara, CA 93103; 805/965-0475; **www.independent means.com**.

On-line Philanthropy:

W. K. Kellogg Foundation Report "E-Philanthropy, Volunteerism and Social Changemaking." This report examines the ways the Internet is being used as a tool for social good; it reports on 140 Web sites, including those promoting volunteering and service and charitable donations. The report is available on-line at **www.WKKF.org**.

Philanthropy Education:

Council of Michigan Foundations K–12 Education in Philanthropy Project. Offers a comprehensive philanthropy curriculum for students in kindergarten through twelfth grade. The curriculum is available through a Web site, and the project also offers teacher training opportunities. 630 Harvey St., Muskegon, MI 49442-2398; 231/767-7206; **http://k12edphil.org**.

The Giving Book: A Young Person's Guide to Giving and Volunteering (three volumes covering separate age groups: 5–8, 9–12 and 13–17). These books are for children but also have instructions and activity ideas parents can use with their children. Order by calling the Milwaukee Foundation, 1020 North Broadway, Milwaukee, WI; 414/290-7350.

Tell Me a Mitzvah: Little and Big Ways to Repair the World by Danny Siegel (Kar-Ben Copies, 1993). Stories of people helping others and suggestions to help readers do their own good deeds. Kar-Ben Copies, 800/452-7236.

The Third Wave Foundation. Hosts an annual young-donors retreat to support, challenge and organize people with wealth aged 15 to 35. 116 E. 16th St., 7th Floor, New York, NY 10003; 212/388-1898; **www.thirdwavefoundation.org**.

Philanthropy Research/Resources:

Council on Foundations. Extensive information and publications to help families create and maintain family foundations or funds at community foundations. 1828 L St., NW, Washington, DC 20036; 202/466-6512; **www.cof.org**.

Indiana University Center on Philanthropy, 550 West North St., Suite 301, Indianapolis, IN 46202-3162; **www.philanthropy. iupui.edu**. The center has produced a number of publications about youth and philanthropy including:

- *The Roots of Giving and Serving* by Richard Bentley and Luana Nissan, 1996. A literature review studying how school-age children learn the philanthropic tradition.

- *Religion, Youth and Philanthropy* by Richard Bentley, Amelie Weber and Cheryl Hall-Russell, 1999. An annotated resource guide of teaching materials used by faith communities to integrate philanthropic values into their education programs for children and youth.

National Center for Family Philanthropy. Helps families and individuals create and sustain their philanthropic missions, regardless of the vehicle. 1220 19th St., NW, Suite 804, Washington, DC 20036; 202/293-3424; **www.ncfp.org**.

Regional Associations of Grantmakers. Members are grantmakers, such as foundations, that partner to enhance the effectiveness of their giving in the regions in which they are located. 1828 L St., NW, Washington, DC 20036; 202/467-0472; **www.rag.org**.

Source Institute. This nonprofit, nonsectarian organization's mission is to advance the well-being of children and youth. It conducts research and develops publications such as:

- *An Asset Builder's Guide to Youth and Money* by Jolene Roehlkepartain, 1999. Covers money management, charitable giving, fundraising and grantmaking.

- *Kids Have a Lot to Give* by Eugene Roehlkepartain, 1999. Shows how congregations can nurture habits of giving and serving for the common good.

Youth Philanthropy: A Framework of Best Practice. Produced by the W. K. Kellogg Foundation, this guidebook shares lessons learned in various youth philanthropy projects. It can be downloaded on-line from **www.WKKF.org**.

Service–Learning in Schools:

Learn and Serve America. A project of the Corporation for National Service, this provides research on service-learning, resources for schools and links to state offices that administer more than 700 programs. 1201 New York Ave., NW, Washington, DC 20525; 202/606-5000; **www.nationalservice.org**.

National Service-Learning Clearinghouse. Part of a collaborative effort to collect and disseminate information for Learn and Serve America programs and other school-based efforts. University of Minnesota, 1954 Buford Ave., St. Paul, MN 55108; 800/808-7378; **www.umn.edu/~serve**.

National Youth Leadership Council. Promotes service-learning programs to engage young people in their schools and communities. Offers training materials to schools and youth leaders. 1910 West County Road B, St. Paul, MN 55113; 651/631-3672; **www.nylc.org**.

Volunteering Opportunities:

America's Promise. Chaired by Gen. Colin Powell, USA, (Ret.) it serves as a catalyst for individuals, organizations and corporations to ensure today's youth grow up to be successful adults. 909 N. Washington St., Suite 400, Alexandria, VA 22314; **www.americaspromise.org**.

City Year. Organizes youth corps to perform community service in cities across the country. 285 Columbus Ave., Boston, MA 02116; 617/927-2500; **www.cityyear.org**.

Do Something Community Connection Campaign. Sponsored by MTV, Pew Charitable Trust and others, this group's Web site connects young people with civic organizations. There's a special emphasis on multicultural activities. Site features celebrity spokespeople and an on-line magazine. 423 W. 55th St., 8th Floor, New York, NY 10019; 212/523-1175; **www.dosomething.org**.

Family Matters. An initiative of the Points of Light Foundation, it links families, neighborhoods, organizations and corporations in volunteer activities. 1400 Eye St., NW, Suite 800, Washington, DC 20005-6526; 202/729-8000; **www.pointsoflight.org**.

FamilyCares. An on-line resource to help families make a difference. The site features dozens of ideas for family projects, with new ones added each month. Membership on the Web site is free, but parents can also obtain information by mail for a small fee. P.O. Box 1083, New Canaan, CT 06840; 914/533-1101; **www. familycares.org**.

Helping.org. Sponsored by the America Online Foundation, this service matches volunteers with jobs by zip code and also lets the site visited make donations to charities.

Kids Care Clubs. A companion project to FamilyCares, this non-profit organization has sparked the creation of more than 400 clubs through which children perform community service projects. The site provides help in organizing a club and offers project ideas and other support. **www.KidsCare.org**.

Prudential Spirit of Community Initiative. In partnership with the Points of Light Foundation and Youth Service America, Prudential teaches young people leadership skills they can apply to community problem solving. Visit the Community Involvement section of the Web site **www.prudential.com**, where you can download a copy of the booklet *Catch the Spirit! A Student's Guide to Community Service*; or obtain one free by calling 973/802-4568.

Roots and Shoots. A project of the Jane Goodall Institute, Roots and Shoots is a global network of children and youth performing environmental and humanitarian efforts. Jane Goodall Institute for Wildlife Research, Education and Conservation, P.O. Box 14890, Silver Spring, MD 20922-4890; 800/592-5263; **www. janegoodall.org**.

VolunteerMatch is a Web-based service that matches volunteers to more than 20,000 jobs nationwide. It also highlights projects volunteers are doing. **www.volunteermatch.org**.

VolunteerAmerica! Helps families find volunteer vacation trips on public lands such as national and state parks and forests. Example: clearing trails in the Grand Canyon. **www.volunteer america.net**.

Youth Service America. Resource center and alliance of 200+ organizations committed to increasing the quality and quantity of opportunities for young people to serve. YSA sponsors National Youth Service Day every April. 1101 15th St., NW, Suite 200, Washington, DC 20005; 202/296-2992; **www.ysa.org**.

Volunteer Recognition:

President's Student Service Awards. Provides certificates and pins to youth who complete a specified number of volunteer hours. Some scholarships are also available for outstanding volunteers. P.O. Box 189, Wilmington, DE 19899-0189; 302/622-9107; **www. student-service-awards.org**.

Prudential Spirit of Community Awards. Given to high school students through the Prudential Youth Leadership Institute (see listing above under Volunteer Opportunities).

About the Author

Susan Crites Price is the coauthor with her husband, Tom, of *The Working Parents Help Book* (Peterson's, 1994, rev. ed. 1996), a guide to juggling family and careers. It won a Parents' Choice Award and was a selection of the Scholastic Book Club. Susan also coauthored *The Complete Idiot's Guide to Child Safety* (Macmillan, 2000).

Susan has been interviewed on *Oprah*, *Today* and numerous other television and radio programs. She also has been interviewed by many newspapers and magazines such as *Parents* and *Working Mother*.

For two years, she and Tom wrote the weekly "Working Parents Lifeline" column, which was distributed by the New York Times Service and published by more than 60 newspapers. Their weekly "Working Solutions" column has been carried by the Family Planet and Disney's Family.com on-line services.

Susan's articles have appeared in such publications as *Working Mother*, *Family Life*, *The Washington Post* and *Washingtonian*, and on several Internet sites.

A freelance writer for the last 15 years, she lives in Washington, DC, with her husband and 15-year-old daughter Julie.